MW01225002

CRICUT
3 BOOKS IN 1

FOR BEGINNERS
DESIGN SPACE
PROJECTS IDEAS

1

BOOK 1 CRICUT FOR BEGINNERS

Table of Contents

BOOK 2   <u>CRICUT DESIGN SPACE</u>

<u>Table of Contents</u>

BOOK 3 <u>CRICUT PROJECTS IDEAS</u>

<u>Table of Contents</u>

CRICUT FOR BEGINNERS

A beginner's guide to cricut designs and crafts. Discover how to work with your machine and realize beautiful creations following pictures and illustrations.

Introduction

If you love crafting, then chances are you have heard about the Cricut machine and all of the wonderful things that you can create with it. If you have heard of the Cricut machine, then you are more than likely thinking of buying one soon. Or, perhaps you obtained one and are now in need of a guide to find out everything about it.

I will help do a quick rundown about the Cricut with the goal that you can see all the wonderful ways to deal with utilize this workstation in your making needs.

Since Cricut started, there are presently a bunch of Cricut machines to choose from. So, which do you need?

All things considered, let me walk you through a differentiation data to give you a chance to find the ideal PC for your assignment needs.

Machine comparison guide

• Maker – Cricut Maker right away and unequivocally cuts more than 300 hundred materials, from the most unobtrusive paper and material to the troublesome stuff like matboard, calfskin, and basswood. Presently your inventive reachable is exponential.

• Explore Air – Performance meets esteem. Cricut Explore Air offers you the expert quality outcomes you need with the additional solace of Bluetooth network for wi-fi cuts and a twofold instrument holder for a messiness free condition.

• The Explore Air Two – Cricut Explore Air two is two times faster than all of the other models. It is able to cut a lot more as well as many other types of material, including iron-on, vinyl, and cardstock.

• Explore One – Cricut Explore One is an astute cutting figuring gadget for DIY activities and specialties that is anything but difficult to break down and simple to utilize. Cut, compose, and rating of 100 materials, for example, cardstock, vinyl, and iron-on.

Cricut Maker

The Cricut Maker is the most up to date propelled Cricut work area, and it has a ton of incredible highlights. They are fundamentally the same as the Explore line; however, they appear to lift a couple of more noteworthy advantages.

• Rotary Blade | They offer a rotating sharp edge that will diminish through material that is unbonded. That capacity you needn't bother with a stabilizer as the Explore machines require.

• Scoring Wheel | This is a pleasant improve from the Scoring Stylus. Spares time and introduces a smooth line.

• Knife Blade | You can utilize this to cut thicker calfskin and even articles like balsa wood, which is top-notch for making. two

• Basic Perforation Blade | Creates best tear-offs and easy strip aways utilizing paper, cardstock, acetic acid derivation, notice board, and that's only the tip of the iceberg

• Wavy Blade | Quickly make a charming wavy zone on a scope of well-known materials.

• Fine Debossing Tip | Customize activities with fresh, specific debossed structures – no envelopes crucial

• Engraving Tip | Engrave uncommon and everlasting structures on a scope of materials.

Cricut moreover presented here in July 2019; there will be a huge amount of new items pushed out available. When I get my hands on them, you can unwind guaranteed this will be your area to desire creates the use of the Cricut line!

Explore Air and Air 2

Both of these machines are a more prominent minimal effort alternative. Explore machines enable you to work with a scope of substances for your creating needs. Vinyl, cardstock, foils, sparkle paper, reinforced texture, and the sky is the limit from there. The biggest distinction between the Explore Air and Air 2 is the size contrast. The Air is a littler additional reduced measurement on the off chance that you don't format to do gigantic tasks, or conceivably have negligible creating space.

Cricut Explore One

Explore One is a work area that I propose to tenderfoots of making.

There are confined aspects anyway adequate that you can make and format exceptional specialties. This is the most reduced rate factor, too, so in the event that you are on a value go, this ought to be a perfect starter machine. At that point, as you study and develop, you can generally improve later to one of the different machines.

Any of the machines are great to claim, it depends on what you format to utilize it for, the zone you have, and what sort of specialties you sketch to utilize.

Which Cricut is best?

1. Cricut Maker | If you need every one of the fancy odds and ends close by with a brisk and calm machine.

2. Explore Air 2 | This is a more noteworthy reasonable processing gadget that comes shut to standing ensuing to the maker rendition!

Cricut has an absolute slew of items and materials. I adore Cricut Infusible Inks and Vinyl Projects; these are likely my top picks. What's more, they make planning easy with Cricut Design Space.

Possibly you got a Cricut work area for Christmas, or a birthday, however, it's as yet sitting in its container. Or on the other hand, maybe you're an eager crafter looking for a straightforward gadget to make making simpler. Or on the other hand, possibly you've considered huge amounts of cool endeavor photos on Pinterest and pondered, "How the hell do they decrease those muddled plans? I wanna do that!" Or maybe you've known about Cricut, yet you're asking, "What is a Cricut machine, and what would you be able to do with it?" Well, you're in the correct spot; today, I will acquaint you with the Cricut Explore Air machine and advise you pretty much all the cool things it can do!

There are no additional cartridges; the entire parcel is done carefully so you can utilize any textual style or structure that is on your PC. The Cricut machines are helpful to utilize, totally adaptable, and exclusively restricted with the guide of your own one of a kind inventiveness!

What is a Cricut Machine?

The Cricut Explore Air is a pass on cutting work area (otherwise known as specialty plotter or cutting machine). You can consider it like a printer; you take a photo or design on your PC and afterward send it to the machine. Then again, rather of printing your plan, the Cricut PC removes it of whatever texture you need! The Cricut Explore Air can cut paper, vinyl, texture, make froth, sticker paper, false cowhide, and that's only the tip of the iceberg! Truth be told, if you like to utilize a Cricut like a printer, it can do that as well! There is a highlight opening in the machine, and you can stack a marker in there, and after that, have the Cricut "draw" your plan for you. It's ideal for getting a top-notch written by hand appear to be if your penmanship isn't too extraordinary. The Explore gathering of Cricut machines favors you to get admission to a monstrous advanced library of "cartridges" rather than utilizing physical cartridges, as I did in school. This implies you can utilize Cricut Design Space (their on-line format programming) to take any content or shape from the library and send it to your Cricut to a. You can even transfer your own plans if you need!

11

The Cricut Explore Air can slice materials up to 12" enormous and has a little diminishing edge introduced inward the machine. At the point when you're prepared to lessen something out, you load the material onto a clingy tangle and burden the tangle into the machine. The tangle holds the fabric set up while the Cricut edge disregards the material and cuts it. At the point when it completes, you dump the tangle from the machine, strip your test off the clingy tangle, and you're outfitted to go!

With a Cricut machine, the odds are perpetual! All you need is a Cricut machine, Design Space, something to cut, and your own innovativeness!

Why it Has Become so Popular Today

The Cricut Maker is the most recent individual from the Cricut Cutting Machine family! two This new workstation is incredible nowadays I'm sharing my Top 10 Reasons You'll adore the Cricut Maker, and it's more prominent than just the marvelous new Cricut ventures you might have the option to make! Truly I have in excess of 10 reasons, and I'll share them as well! From paper and vinyl to wooden and texture, there is no shortage of considerations and substances you can make!

You remember we cherish the Cricut Explore Air 2 for all its top-notch cutting and creating capacities. Well presently meet monstrous sister, and she's solid and inventive and prepared to make all the Cricut activities into the late evening! (Or on the other hand, till you come up short on coffee and head to sleep). The Cricut maker is the Cricut Explore with an all-out new arrangement of abilities. I believe you're going to love her! These Reasons Will Have You Cherishing Cricut. The Cricut Maker decreasing machine is fast, fantastic, and furnished to work with Texture! I was competent to see it live and face to face at an ongoing occasion facilitated by method for the Cricut group in Salt Lake City. The issues you have come to adore about the Cricut Explore family are all together in any case there. Presently there's even extra to cherish. I'm giving both of you records. They are really a similar rundown, anyway for these you that resemble me and pick a snappy answer at this moment, I have the best 11 brisk reasons. For completely every other person that needs the intricate details and the how's and whys, I'm clarifying more prominent about each component. How about we go!

The Best 11 Reasons Why You'll Fall in Love With Cricut

1.   Same reasonable yet better! – The same machine at the center with more highlights, power, and challenge conceivable outcomes

2.   Cuts material – New sharp edge, venture examples and tangle all planned particularly for developing with texture

3.   Sewing Examples from Effortlessness – 100's of sewing designs reachable in Configuration Space (with crease remittances)

4.   Turning Sharp edge – to cut material and a wide range of sensitive materials

5.   Blade Sharp edge – to decrease overwhelming duty materials like balsa and birchwood

6.   Versatile Apparatus Framework – to take into consideration additional diminishing control and more noteworthy gadget additional items later on

7.   More Stockpiling – the special Explore stockpiling is new and extended to give more noteworthy choices

8.   Print on Shaded paper – print on hued and designed paper with print-then-cut plans

9.   Gadget holder and charger – a region on the apex of the PC to hold your units and a charging port so you can cost while you make

10.   iOs and Android applications – the two iOs and Android clients can make in a hurry!

11.   Wonderful Plan Subtleties – same dazzling portrayal with brought little print and only a bit more prominent than the one of a kind Explore.

<u>Top 11 Reasons – The Detailed List</u>

If the short posting above sufficiently wasn't, here is my more prominent little print to see why you'll cherish these new components secured in the Cricut Maker. It's a dazzling PC with adequate flexibility and capacity to help make the undertakings you like to make. From paper artworks to little carpentry extends, this work area can make such a large number of particular plans and activities with you!

1.   The same magnificent PC is, however, shockingly better! – alright, this really is anything but another "reason" to cherish another machine. Aside from me, it is the additional fundamental reason I cherish this new machine. I, as of now, love my Cricut Explore Air 2. I cherish the use of Configuration Space, and I'm in all actuality satisfied with all the imaginative energizing I can have with this device. The Cricut Maker is only that, however far and away superior. There are more prominent highlights, additional abilities, moves up to things I as of now love

15

and new things to attempt. Continue examining, and you'll understand.

2.   Cricut Maker cuts material – the new Cricut Maker has been re-engined to work with texture. It comes outfitted and arranged to make with another rotary cutting edge and explicit fabric one of a kind tangle. You study that right... texture! Presently, I perceive a few people have been cutting texture with their Cricut machines. I haven't had a lot of favorable luck with it. I've typically wanted to diminish fabric that I can use in my sewing venture, appliques, designs, and so on. Presently the Cricut Maker has been sketched to do just that! I tried the cutting abilities, and they are delightful. The same simply follows you'd foresee in the event that you cut by methods for the hand! Not a sewist? Forget about it! Crafters can join understanding that there is no texture we cannot create with the use of our Cricuts well, almost all materials. I haven't found one yet that I cannot cut.

3.   Sewing Examples from Effortlessness in Configuration Space

4.   Rotational Sharp edge –Not exclusively does this sharp edge cut texture pleasantly, it will likewise be you're a fine companion for cutting refined materials. I hear it will decrease

crepe paper splendidly! So, think. You're never again simply compelled to extravagant cardstock and specialty papers. We should test with every one of the substances from tissue paper to balsawood – the Cricut can adapt to it!

5.   Blade Sharp edge – Cut thicker substances with the new blade edge. Cut balsa wood or birchwood, or what about thicker cardboard or even chipboard. Presently your imagination can go even likewise with more noteworthy materials and cut alternatives!

6.   Versatile Device Framework – so you, as of now, analyze that the new Cricut Maker accompanies a rotating edge, and a blade cutting edge will rapidly be accessible. Things more decisions to come. This new Cricut machine has been intended to empower more prominent hardware as the group envisions additional gear to make. So, as they assume up additional approaches to enable you to make, the PC is set up for new hardware to be included... you'll simply need to sit back and watch what's straightaway!

7.   More Stockpiling – The pen holder on the Maker has been overhauled to protect extra of your instruments and embellishments. There is a profound cup and a shallow cup to get admission to a scope of things effectively. Also, the in-

entryway complement holder has furthermore been overhauled to comprise of a couple of additional compartments. All your Cricut adornments have a home!

8.   Print on Shaded paper – What!? Truly, it is valid. The print-then-cut capacity is matched with the Cricut Maker to take into account imprinting on shaded and designed paper. You never again are limited to printing your Cricut structures on white paper. So proceed, get imaginative and print layers of workmanship and lessen your somewhat plans with extra breathtaking shading!

9.   Gadget holder and charger – We utilize our versatile units to make with our Cricut machines, and now the Maker has a district to put those gadgets while we chip away at our undertakings. Set your phone or work area in the device holder at the apex of the machine. What's more, there is a USB port on the Maker so you can connect your gadget and charge it while you are making. helpful, I state!

10.   iOs AND Android applications – You can set up your cut plans from anyplace with the cell applications helpful for the two iOs and Android. Effectively make the formats you want to make on your iPhone and keep for later at that point finish on your PC. You can ship plans to cut legitimate from the cell application or

keep to your Structure Space account and get the right portion to it later.

11.　　　Delightful Plan Subtleties – really, the design is considerably prettier, and the measurement is marginally greater with the Cricut Maker. In any case, presently, not a horrendous parcel greater. The Cricut Maker will, by and by fit in your conveying case and should, in any case, fit on your favored art rack. They've also ensured some additional extravagant bling and finishing.

What Is A Cricut Machine?

The generic title for the Cricut is a die cutter, craft plotter, or a smart cutting machine. The format of this machine allows you to create projects from flat materials of varying thicknesses. The projects that you can do with this tool can range from simple to quite complex, depending on your skill level with these materials. Depending on the sharpness of the blade in your cutting machine, or the model that you're using, your materials can range anywhere from craft felt to thin sheets of metal. This gives you an idea of how vast the range really is, for what this machine can help you to accomplish as a crafter.

Other machines of this type can run you several hundred or even thousands of dollars, require design degrees, come with complex proprietary software, and offer only a fraction of the design options that come with Cricut, and the proprietary, user-friendly Cricut Design Space. Cricut's massive base of users are always sharing the latest and greatest in projects, tips, tricks, guides, and new materials to use with your Cricut machine. As a crafter with a Cricut machine, your resources are nearly limitless.

Thanks to the vast number of resources at our disposal as crafters, I've decided to compile the best of what's available, so you don't have to sift through anything confusing before getting started making your gorgeous projects and loving your new Cricut machine. In one organized place, you'll be able to access all the information you need on how to use the software, project guides that take you from start to finish, a list of all that you will need, and so much more. This is your comprehensive guide that you can refer to again and again, no matter how your skill level grows over time!

Just like with many other crafting media, if you're not paying attention, it is possible to spend more than you intended on materials, tools, accessories, and more. My intention is to show you which proprietary tools are worth the extra money, while showing you the best alternatives that you can use in place of other tools. Crafting is such a therapeutic and enjoyable experience; it shouldn't be prohibitive thanks to the cost! As you gain familiarity with the community of Cricut users, with the Cricut brand, I'm confident you will find the products and tricks that work the best for you in bringing your crafts to life!

Let's dive into how to choose the right Cricut model for you and for your needs!

How Can I Choose the Right Model for Me?

The wonderful thing about Cricut is that their models are all incredibly versatile and capable. Most capabilities that are had by one model will span the entire current Cricut line of products. There are some very minor differences in the ways in which they work and the complexity of their operation.

What's Available?

Thankfully, there is not a vast number of craft plotters available from Cricut at the time of writing, which means it will be really easy for you to take a look at all of what's offered without being overwhelmed. With huge product lines that contain many various models, finding what you want and need, while getting the most for your money can be a real chore. I'll outline each of the models currently available, what they can do, and what capabilities are best suited for what types of crafts.

Cricut Explore One

In terms of what is currently available from Cricut, this is the most basic machine they offer. This machine boasts being able to cut 100 of the most popular materials that are currently available to use with your Cricut machine, as well as being perfectly user friendly.

The Cricut Explore One is considered to be the no-frills beginner model of Cricut craft plotters and operates at a lower speed than the other models available. Unlike the others available in the current product line, the Cricut Explore One has only one accessory clamp inside, so cutting or scoring, and drawing cannot be done simultaneously. They can, however, be done in rapid succession, one right after the other.

While this is a great tool for a wide range of crafts on 100 different materials, and which can get you well on your way to designing breathtaking crafts that are always a cut above others, the cost is not as high as you might imagine. If you intend to use your craft plotter mainly for those special occasions where something handcrafted would be perfect, then this a great machine to have on hand.

At the time of writing this, the cost for the Cricut Explore One is $179.99

Cricut Explore Air

With all the capabilities of the Cricut Explore One and more, the Cricut Explore Air model comes equipped with Bluetooth capability, has a built-in storage cup to keep your tools in one place while you're working, so they won't roll away or get lost in the shuffle.

This model does have two on-board accessory clamps, which allow for simultaneous marking and cutting or scoring. These clamps are marked with an A and a B so you can be sure your tools are going in the right places, every time you load them in.

This model is equipped to handle the same 100 materials as the Cricut Explore One, and operates at the same speed, so the price difference reflects those differences and the similarities! This is a great value for the powerhouse that you're getting.

At the time of writing this, the cost for the Cricut Explore Air is $249.99

Cricut Explore Air 2

The Cricut Explore Air 2 is Cricut's current top selling craft plotter and is arguably the best value they have to offer for the price. This model cuts materials at twice the speed of the other two models, has Bluetooth capability, and has the two on-board accessory clamps.

The storage cup on the top of the machine features a secondary, more shallow cut to store your replacement blade housings when they're not in use, so that if you happen to be swapping between several different tips for a project, they're all readily available to you throughout your project. Both of the cups have a soft silicone bottom, so you won't have to worry about the blades on your machine becoming dull or scratched!

For someone who finds themselves using their Cricut with any regularity, this is the best machine for the job. You will be able to do your crafts twice as fast, and you will get a satisfactory result every time, even at that speed!

At the time of writing, the Cricut Explore Air 2 is priced exactly the same as the Cricut Explore One, at $249.99. If you're looking to jump on this, now is the time to get the best deal.

Cricut Maker

The Cricut Maker is considered to be Cricut's flagship model. This is the one that can do just about anything under the sun on just about any material you can fit into the mat guides of your machine. The one drawback of this powerhouse model is the price point. This does make this model more prohibitive, unless you plan to make crafts that you can sell with this model. If this is your intention, you can rest assured that whatever you turn out with this machine will be the best of the best, every single time. If you're selling your crafts, this baby will pay for itself in little to no time at all.

For the avid crafter who likes to show up to the party with the most gorgeous crafts that are leaps and bounds ahead of their peers, this machine might be overkill for the price. Of course, if you are keeping up with the Joneses, this is the model to have.

This model really does have it all and we can prove it. No other Cricut machine has the speed that the Cricut Maker has. The cuts that can be made with the special precision blades that fit only this machine, are crisper than anything you could ever hope for from a straight knife or other craft cutter. The blade housings allow you to simply remove the tip from the housing, install the next one, clip it back into place, and keep on rolling through your projects. In addition to this, the machine can detect the material loaded into it, so you won't need to set the type of materials at the beginning of each of your projects. With the other model, a common occurrence is that the project is halfway done before the crafter realizes that the dial is set incorrectly.

The machine, like some of the others, is fully Bluetooth capable, it operates with ten times as much power as any of the other models, it has a special rotary cutter attachment that allows it to glide effortlessly through fabrics and precision, and so much more.

At the time of writing, the Cricut Maker is priced at $399.99

Are There Older Models?

In a word, yes. There are several older models that have been phased out to make way for the Explore and Maker machines. The older machines were found to require a good deal more hacks, workarounds, troubleshooting, and understanding to get precise or even rounded cuts for the projects that crafters would like to do.

Here is a list of some of the models you may have seen in your travels:

- Personal Cricut Electronic Cutter Machine
- Cricut Create
- Expression 1
- Expression 2
- Imagine
- Cricut Mini
- Cricut Explore

Each of these models was compatible with a Cricut product called the Gypsy, which was not unlike the Cricut Design Space that we currently have today. Each of these machines had its triumphs in innovating the craft cutting processes.

The major aspect that Cricut aimed for overhauling when creating their newest line of models, was the complexity involved in working with their machinery. Communities of crafters had come together with hacks and math ledgers to program their machinery to work precisely as they wanted it to.

With the current line of available models, the Cricut Design Space allows you to be an innovative as you can possibly be with the design process, so none of your creative flow is eaten up by operations that should be taken care of by your machine.

If you own one of these machines, updating is certainly worth the money, but if it has served you well in your crafting, there is no need to upgrade. Cricut has always made quality products, and the cartridges containing various themed design elements are still supported through Cricut Design Space.

The Cricut Cartridge Adapter is a USB adapter, which allows you to import your cartridges into the Cricut Design Space, so all your elements are available in one organized space.

How To Use Cricut Machine

One of the greatest things about a Cricut is that it is extremely simple to use. It takes a while to get used to using it, but once you get the hang of it, only your creativity is the limit. Firstly, what comes with your Cricut? That depends on what product you purchase and the money you pay. The more you pay, the more you get.

These don't look like a lot of things, but they are all the right ones to get you started. For a beginner, it is recommended that you purchase a starter set which includes the necessary accessories.

Setting Up the Machine

The first step in the process of setting up a Cricut is to determine where the machine will be best located. Ideally, the machine will be placed near a computer or tablet, a power source and where it has room to work. Even if the machine does not require to be hooked to a computer, try to keep it within reach to make the process of loading and unloading easier.

The installation of a newer Cricut machine can be done in minimal steps. After the completion of all the installation steps you will start out with a free trial of Cricut Access, which gives

29

access to additional projects, images. This trail cannot be paused so make sure you optimize the time of the trail.

To begin:

• Turn on the machine after it is connected to the power source.

• Use Bluetooth or the USB cable to connect the machine to the computer or your device.

• To set up a Cricut on a Mac or Window's computer;

• Go to the website for setup: https://design.cricut.com/setup

• If you do not have a Cricut.com account, create one to log in, or use your account information to log into Cricut.com

• When prompted, the Design Space plug-in should be downloaded and installed on the computer.

• Cricut Access will ask for acceptance of the terms of use to activate the free trial.

• When the prompt to make the first cut appears to set up is complete.

If you have any problems or the instructions are not clear; I highly advise you to visit the main Cricut website on how to setup your machine: http://help.cricut.com/help/manuals

Make Sure There's Space

The Cricut has to be set up with a space at the back of the machine as well as the front so that the mat can move freely as the blade cuts away. The risk of having your project fall to the floor if you do not have enough room in front and you are unloading is too big for comfort; that's why I prefer to be safe rather than be sorry. Keep that in mind when giving your Cricut its new home. There also needs to be space above your machine as you will have to open and close the lid to replace the blades, put in your markers and stylus, and work the buttons. Make sure that you do not stuff it in a tiny little shelf because that will end badly, I can assure you of that.

Opening and Checking

You can now open the box, breathe in, enjoy that new toy, and relish that butterfly feeling in your tummy whenever you take goodies out of the box. As with every new thing that you purchase, ensure that everything you ordered has arrived and that nothing is damaged. While this is a tedious step, no one wants broken items, especially since you are so excited to craft.

Placing and Taking the First Step

Once you have confirmed that everything is in an excellent condition, you can place your Cricut on its rightful area. The bottom will then drop slowly, leaving your machine open. Next, you can remove the foam packaging from inside the machine. You will notice that there are two clamps in the tool holder that had foam stuck to it. One is labeled "A," while the other one is labeled "B." Ensure that the blade is already in its clamp that is labeled "B," which stands for blade. "A" is for the accessories, e.g., your markers.

Following the Link

There will be a link on a piece of paper that you got with your box, which will take you through every step, ensuring that you setup your Cricut machine correctly. After following the guideline, you will then need to plug your power cable into both the Cricut and the power outlet. Congratulations - your Cricut is now alive!

Connecting to Your Computer

Now, you can turn on your machine.To connect the unit that requires the cable to your laptop, you simply have to put the square end in its designated place at the back of your Cricut and attach the rectangular end to the USB port on your desktop or Laptop.

If you have a wireless device, enable your Bluetooth on whichever device you wish to connect your Cricut to, open the

Bluetooth settings, and pair with the machine. You will instantly recognize the name of your machine. Now, you're all set!

Cricut Software

- Design Space

Design Space is for any Explore machine with a high-speed, broadband Internet connection that is connected to a computer or an iOS device. This more advanced software allows full creative control for users with Cricut machines.

- Craft Room

Some machines, such as the Explore and Explore Air, cannot use Craft Room, but many other models can. Craft Room users also have access to a free digital cartridge, which offers images that all Cricut machines can cut.

Moving on to Creating Your Project Template

On the home page, select "New Project", which will be followed by a page with a blank canvas that looks like the grid on your Cricut mats. To any artist, the words "empty canvas" is a nightmare in itself so please just bear with me since we will fill that bad boy up in a second. But first, let's go through the menu options.

New, Templates, Projects, Images, Text, Shapes, and Upload. These are the things that you will see on your left-hand side when you have the canvas open on the screen.

Cricut Basic

This is a program or software designed to help the new user get an easy start on designing new crafts and DIY projects. This system will help you with image selection to cutting with the least amount of time spent in the design stages. You can locate your image, pre-set projector font, and immediately print, cut, score, and align with tools that are found within the program. You can use this program on the iOS 7.1.2 or later systems as well as iPad and several of the iPhones from the Mini to the 5th generation iPod touch. Since it is also a cloud-based service, you are able to start in one device and finish from another.

Sure Cuts a Lot

This is another third-party software that has a funny name which gives you the ability to take control of your designs without some of the limitations that can happen when using cartridges used within the Cricut DesignStudio. You will need to install an update to your software to use this program; you can download it for free. It allows for the use of TrueType and OpenType font formats as well as simple drawing and editing tools. You can import any file format and then convert to the one that you need. There is an option for blackout and shadow.

Cricut DesignStudio

This program allows you to connect with your software and provides you with much more functionality as far as shapes and fonts are concerned. There are various options for tools that provide you resources for designing more creative images. You will be able to flip, rotate, weld, or slant the images and fonts. However, you will still be limited in the amounts or types of fonts that you can use based on the ones on the cartridges. There is a higher level of software features that allow for customization.

Cricut Sync

This is a program designed for updating the Cricut Expression 2 as well as the Imagine machine and the Gypsy device. You just connect your system to the computer and run the synced program for an installation of updates on the features that come with your machine. This is also used to troubleshoot many issues that could arise from the hardware.

Play Around and Practice

You can combine your shapes and images, add some text, and create patterns. The possibilities are endless. The best thing to do is familiarize yourself with the software before you attempt on cutting expensive materials. Start small and cheap - printer paper will be an ideal choice - and cut away. See what works well for you and stick with it. There are many options concerning the Cricut Design Space, and the only way to learn all of this is to experiment and click on every tab you see and try different combinations of options when playing around on the software.

Make the Cut

This is a third-party program that works with the Cricut design software. It offers a straightforward look at the design features that Cricut has. This system can convert a raster image into a vector so that you can cut it. There is also a great way to do lattice tools. It uses many file formats and TrueType fonts. There are advanced tools for editing and an interface that is easy to learn and use. This system works with Craft ROBO, Gazelle, Silhouette, Wishblade, and others. It allows you to import any file from a TTF, OTF, PDF, GSD, and so on and convert them to JPG, SVG, PDF, and so on. It is flexible and user-friendly.

Dials, Blades, and Settings

The speed, size, and pressure dials are the dials used to customize settings to various materials. For instance, if the material is thinner less pressure is needed from the blade than with a thicker material. On many machines, there is a Smart Set Dial. This is a setting that eliminates the need to customize speed, size, and pressure for each different material. Whether you are cutting card stock, vinyl, or fabric, etc. the Smart Set Dial setting will put the blade in the correct position for cutting. It is a great idea to buy many blades of various depth cuts. Thicker materials like leather, thicker card, and more require a deep cut blade which can be found at the Cricut shop at cricut.com. Currently, there are five available blades. The first is the fine point blade; this blade is used primarily for light to medium materials like paper, card stock, and vinyl. The fine point blade is a gold color. The fine point blade comes with the Cricut Explore One, Cricut Explore Air, and Cricut Explore Air 2. The next blade is the deep point blade, which is used for thick materials such as chipboard, foam sheets, and very thick card stock, etc. Thirdly, the Bonded Fabric Blade is used to optimally cut fabric that is bonded with the backing material. Next is the Rotary Blade. The Rotary Blade is not sold individually but it does come with the Cricut Maker and can cut any type of fabric. The Rotary Blade can cut fabric that is not bonded with backing paper, unlike the Bonded Fabric Blade. Like the Rotary Blade, the final blade is exclusive to the Cricut Maker and cuts stronger woods like basswood but is sold separately from the Maker. Whichever blade you choose to use make sure that the blade is Cricut brand.

Using a non-Cricut brand blade can cause the machine to not cut properly. On many different blogs, there will be an example chart that shows which settings to use with each material. Even when using the settings from the chart try to do test cuts before the final cut to make sure that the settings are correct. Just like you would use cheap material like printer paper to do your first cut with your machine you should also use cheap material to do test cuts just in case something goes wrong.

Loading and Unloading Paper

The Cricut Cutter machine comes with a Standard Grip Cutting mat, but some materials require a lighter or stronger grip. To the right is a guide to show which strength mat you need to use for each material. Also, be sure to place the material or paper where the "Align Paper Corner Here" icon is. Placing the paper anywhere else on the cutting mat will either prevent cutting or cause a malfunction in the cutting process. The Cricut Cutter machine should load the mat and the material at that time if it does not select the Unload Paper button on the keypad and retry the process. When cutting materials do not attempt to cut on material smaller than three inches by three inches on all models except the Cricut Mini. The recommended size for cutting is six inches by twelve inches, especially for your first try cutting with the Cricut Cutter machine. It is also recommended to practice on cheap materials when first cutting to get the hang of using your Cricut Cutter machine. Although it can be expensive, it is suggested to keep many different materials on hand of various prices and thickness so that when you want to execute a project you already have the materials on hand. In addition, the Cricut Cutter machine comes with a Sample Project. Many Cricut masters and bloggers suggest that this be your first project. Trying to do a complicated project the first go around is not an intelligent or safe decision. Once you are done cutting select the Unload Paper key and take out the cutting mat. From there, slowly peel off the material or paper to avoid rips and damage to your creation; then peel away all excess material from the cut-out. The first time using the cutting mat can be difficult because the brand-new mat can be extremely sticky. It is a good tip to de-tack your cutting mat by placing a t-shirt on the sticky mat to get rid of a bit of the stick ness of the mat. Not doing this step increases the probability of destroying your creation when peeling it off of the cutting mat. Another quick tip is when removing access material from a very small design or intricate design use a lint roller. Roll the lint roller over the top of the design cutout to remove every little piece of material. When removing the cut out from the cutting mat use a scraping tool. Basic tools do not come with your Cricut Cutter machine, but they are quite useful tools and it is recommended to invest in the tools which can be bought at cricut.com. (Tools to use include the Cricut Blade, Hook, Scoop, and Scraping tools). Make sure to always remove all paper and or material from the cutting mat after each creation is made. Doing these steps ensures that the cutting mat will be fantastic at performing later. Also, it is recommended to keep the plastic covering that the cutting mat comes with. Put the plastic covering back onto the mat when finished cutting to keep the mat clean.

To recap, put the paper onto the cutting mat; then select load paper. Once the mat is inside select the cut button then presses unload paper when the cut is finished.

Selecting Shapes, Letters, and Phrases

However, in order for the cut to be made the machine must know what to cut. To tell your Cricut Cutter machine what to cut select the shapes, letters, and/or phrases you would like to cut out up to sixteen items. Whatever items you select should appear on your LCD display screen. Now that you know a few basic operations it is best to learn the functions of a few of the keys and buttons located on the keypad at the top of the machine.

Keys and Buttons on Keypad

Do not hold the shift button; it is only necessary to select the button then select the key with the shape or letter on the upper right corner that you would like. That shape or letter should then appear on the LCD display screen. When the shift key is activated it will be lit up.

The Shift lock key does the exact same thing as the Shift key except the Shift lock key allows for the repeated selection of upper right corner shapes and letters without having to keep selecting the shift key. Space and backspace keys work the exact same as space and backspace keys on a keyboard on a computer or other digital device. The space key puts a blank space between the two letters, shapes, or words. The backspace key deletes the last letter, shape or word selected from the LCD display screen. Most Cricut users do not use the space key as they cut one word at a time. It is recommended to use the space key when negative space in the cut is desired.

The Clear Display key, unlike the backspace key, will delete all selected shapes, letters, and phrases from the LCD Display screen. The Reset All key erases all settings on your Display screen returning all the settings to the factory default.

Create An Account On "Cricut.Com" And "Cricut Access"

"Cricut" is poised to become a one stop shop for all your crafting and DIY project ideas. Their "Design Space" application is developed to let the artist inside you flourish into the world of technological advancements. It is a free and easy-to-learn design software that can work with all kinds of "Cricut" devices. It is also a cloud-based application, which allows you to seamlessly access all your design files from any device whenever you need it.

The software is synchronized across your devices so you can start a project on your mobile phone when the inspiration strikes and pick it right up from your laptop. It also supports the integrated camera on your devices so you can view your designs on real-life backgrounds. You can then wirelessly connect the "Design Space" with your "Cricut Explore" or "Cricut Maker" to easily print and cut your designs.

Here are some of the amazing features offered by "Cricut Design Space":

- Seamlessly design and cut all your crafts with any of the "Cricut Explore" and "Cricut Maker" machines.

- Wide variety of selection from over 50k pictures, fonts and projects through the "Cricut Image Library". And you can also upload your own pictures and fonts absolutely free of any charge to create personalized designs.

- You will also be able to edit and enhance your uploaded pictures to take your projects to the next level.

- This application allows you to download pictures and fonts on your devices so you can continue designing and cutting your project even with no Internet.

- The "Make It Now" projects are carefully crafts so you easily design your ideas and quickly cut the any of the pre-designs, when you are running short on time.

- You can create decorations for holiday and party, cards, wedding invitations, scrapbooks, fashionable accessories and jewelry, personalized crafts for babies and kids, and the list goes on and on.

- By connection with "Cricut" machines, you can easily cut a range of different materials such as "paper, vinyl, iron-on, cardstock, poster board, fabric and even thicker materials like leather".

- You can create an account on "Cricut" for free and sign in with your "Cricut ID" to work on your fonts, pictures and projects. It would even let's you easily pay for any purchase made on "Cricut.com" or directly within "Design Space".

- The "Cricut" machines and "Design Space" support Bluetooth connectivity so your can wirelessly connect the software with your machines. However, some machine may require "wireless Bluetooth adapter" that you can easily purchase online.

Creating an account on "Cricut.com"

Now that you understand what "Design Space" is and how you can use to create beautiful DIY projects. Let's look at how you can get your own "Cricut ID" to log into the "Design Space" application.

1. On the official "Cricut" site, select *"Design"* from the top right corner of the screen.

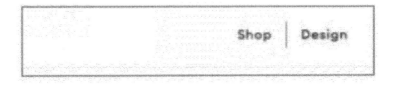

2. A new window will open, from the bottom of the screen select *"Create A Cricut ID"*.

Sign in with your Cricut ID

Email / Cricut ID

Password

Enter your password

Forgot?

☐ Remember me

Don't have an account yet?

Create A Cricut ID

3. *Now, in the window as shown in the picture below, you would need to enter your personal information, such as, first name, last name, email ID and*

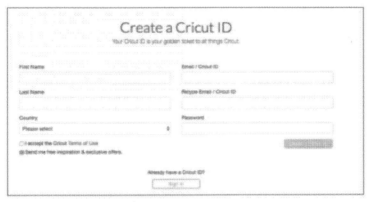

password.

4. You would then need to check the box next to "*I accept the Cricut Terms of Use*" and click on "*Create a Cricut ID*".

5. You will be instantly taken to the "Design Space" landing page and a message reading *"New! Set your machine mode"* will be displayed.

With the steps above you have registered your email address as your new "Cricut ID"!!!!

Now, let's see how you can complete your registration and start using "Design Space".

1. When you log into "Design Space" for the first time, your screen will display the message as shown in the picture below.

2. Click on *"Next"* as displayed in the picture above, a blacked out screen with *"Machine"* on the top right

corner of the screen will be displayed as shown in the picture below.

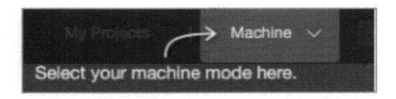

3. Click on *"Machine"* and the options of the "Cricut" machines will be displayed as shown below.

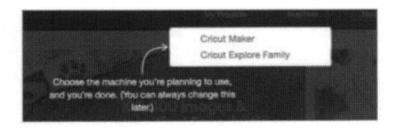

4. You can select your device from the two options. For this example, "Cricut Maker" was selected and

upon selection, the next screen will confirm the device you selected, as shown in the picture below.

Remember, if you wish to toggle to the "Cricut Explore", all you have to do is click on the "Maker" and you will see the drop down option for the two machines again, as shown in the picture below.

Design Space on Mobile Devices

As mentioned earlier, the "Cricut Design Space" is cloud based and you can pick up your project across various platforms. Here's how you can download the latest version (v 3.18.1) of this application on your mobile devices.

Apple App Store (iOS) – Simply search for "Cricut" on the App store from your iPhone or iPad and select "GET" to begin the download. You can then easily login with your registered "Cricut ID" to continue working on your projects on your phone.

Google Play (Android) – You can search for "Cricut" on the Google Play from your android phone and table. Then select "Install" to begin the download. Once completed use your "Cricut ID" to login and pick up your projects and ideas where you left off.

Accessories And Tools

When you have a Cricut machine, there are a few tools that you would need which would make your crafting project easier and manageable. All these different tools help with cutting materials. The tools that you would need are:

Cricut Cutting Mat

For every Cricut Machine you have, the must-have item every crafter need is a cutting mat. This cutting mat enables you to hold any material you use while the machine goes through cutting it. These mats come in different grip strength and varying sizes. You can differentiate it by the colors it comes in based on the grip, so you do not confuse them. Some projects would require you to use the StrongGrip mat, whereas some projects work better using a mat suitable based on the materials you are using, such as fabric.

The outcome of your project depends on the kind of mat you use so choosing the right mat is imperative. The different types of mats available are the LightGrip Mat, StandardGrip Mat, StrongGrip Mat, and the FabricGrip Mat.

Cricut Bright Pad

This Bright Pad includes a five-brightness setting adjustable LED light. It makes your crafting easier, and it aids in illuminating extremely fine lines for tracing. It is extremely useful when you are weeding so if you do find that weeding is a challenge, then the Cricut Bright Pad will solve this issue for you as it makes this process easier.

Cricut Pens

Cricut Pens come in different colors and a variety of sets that make DIY projects such as gift tags, cards, invitations, and banners so much more creative and beautiful. Crafters usually use these pens when they need to Write and Cut. You can get the Metallic pens, Candy Shop pens, the Classic set, Gold set, and even one called the Seaside set.

Lint Roller

Yes, you read that right, get yourself a lint roller. It is useful for removing any unwanted pet hairs, dust or excess materials from your mats. Animal hairs are big problems as they stick to the adhesive mats like there is no tomorrow, but a lint roller works great if you want to get rid of them.

Scoring Stylus

Add a scoring stylus to your cart as soon as possible if you are a paper crafter. The tool is excellent for making paper baskets and boxes. It gives the products the professional, store-bought finish and makes them so easy to fold as the stylus already creates the grooves for folding your paper projects.

EasyPress

Invest in an EasyPress. This is perfect if you are interested in printing T-shirts or customizing pillowcases. Basically, anything you want to have printed; you are going to need one of these bad boys to do it. There are lots of bundles available on the Cricut website, and they can range from $119.99 (only the EasyPress) to $389.99 for a large bundle with everything you need to get started on your printing journey and so much more. The prices change depending on the size of the EasyPress, as well as the size of the bundle you wish to take.

Complete Starter Kit

The Complete Starter Kit is great if you don't feel like purchasing tools individually or if you'd rather follow protocol and purchase exactly what you need. The kit comes with all the essential items; that's why it is a great purchase. However, if you're tight on cash, buying the bare necessities will be best. This includes the materials you may require starting crafting so you don't have to worry about any list of items that need to be bought.

Cartridge

Cartridges are designed to help with the keyboard overlay that is needed for designs. The DesignStudio that is downloadable on the computer will help with developing the design that you are looking for. Each cartridge is designed to have a booklet to help you with how to use it. Each cartridge will only work for that specific overlay; however, a company called Provo Craft designed a universal overlay cartridge that will help with this single use overlay issue. This allows the DIY crafter to only must learn one keyboard overlay instead of multiple, giving them a much better chance of being able to learn the Cricut machine easily. Each Cricut, whether a cake version or a paper version, has a specific set of parameters that will be set to use for cutting. This makes each one of the Cricut machines specific to their use and a unique tool to have.

Buy a cartridge or several. Please do invest in these. They are amazing, and they aren't that expensive if you look around for clearance sales or marked-down prices on Amazon. There are so many cartridges to choose from; it's like a never-ending pit of creativity. The selection ranges from themed cartridges to ones that only have fonts. It's great for any project, and it saves you the trouble of struggling with Design Space and creating your own designs. They also come in neat little boxes that are so easy to store and always looks uniform.

Sharpies

Sharpies - you will not be sorry that you have them. Yes, the Cricut pens are cool, but they are overpriced. Purchasing some extra Sharpies – or any form of pens that can be manipulated into fitting into the pen holder – will work perfectly. You will have a variety of colors and save a couple of bucks in the process.

Doors

The door on your Cricut Cutter machine protects the machine when not in use. On many Cricut Cutter machines in various models, there is a compartment on the inside of the door to place any needed tools for crafting. If the doors on your Cricut cutter machine are not staying shut, make sure that you have taken out or unloaded any accessories in the machine's accessory clamp which can cause the doors to remain open.

Spatula

For lifting cut peace of papers from the cutting mat spatula is used. Other related things like some stuffed card can be used.

But, as spatula is not expensive and specially designed tool, so its use is recommended. It does not harm your cutting mat. Removing gross and sticky material from spatula is easy.

Adhesives

Glue, gums are adhesives, choose adhesive of your choice from any well-known brand. Sticky material like adhesives should not be ordinary, purpose of sticking two things together must be fulfilled through your selected adhesive. Different sizes of glue coffee cups are available. Select any jumbo pack or coffee cup or according to your requirement. The drying time of glue also matters, so go for some very good adhesive.

Tapes

Without tape completing task is almost impossible. Consideration Points for selecting tape are it should be chemical or acid free and it should be very sticky. Glue is alternate for tape, but sometime glue also does not work like tape.

Scissors

Keep a pair of sharp scissors with you. Enough sharp to cut cards, ribbons and papers. Must buy a cover for scissors. Place it above the reach of children and in a place where humidity does not affect it. Neat paper or card cutting really affect your decorative work.

Tweezers

Sometimes you need to deal with very tiny papers. Tweezers work efficiently in holding that small piece of papers which usually turns, curves and torn during use. Sometime additional use of glue sticks two papers which are difficult to get separate tweezers are perfect helper at that time. Keep it while doing crafting you will be needing it.

Trimmers

Blades and trimmers are essential thing it helps in cutting papers very neatly and in desired shape without putting additional effort to create neat effect.

Stock of paper and cards Card are comparatively thicker than paper. They are different things. Buying a stock makes you tension free, either you do test cuttings or throw it in making unusual shapes for trail. They should be enough for, until your whole tasks get complete.

Blades

The blades are designed to cut specific textiles when using the Cricut. Every single Cricut machine that you can buy comes with your own specific blade for that machine. You can purchase other blades that would be even more useful for specific textiles. Many of them come with a German fine point carbide blade. This is a useful blade for all projects. However, you may want to invest in a deep cut blade eventually. This one provides an effortless cutting of a much thicker textile such as leather and wood. There is an individual housing that will be used for this specific blade that is different from the one that comes with your machine, so keep that in mind. There is also an option or a fabric blade that is bonded. This is used to cut fabrics that are already stabilized with some sort of heat-pressed bonding. In the Cricut Maker, you will get a knife blade and a rotary as well. These do not work in other Cricut machines though.

Keypad

The keypad allows you to input phrases and words to tell the Cricut what to cut out using the font in the cartridge.

Buttons

For the most part, all buttons are self-explanatory the on button turns the machine on, the Cut button tells the machine to Cut once the design is already in place, and the Stop button tells the Cricut machine to stop cutting once the design has been fully cut. It is important to not try to Cut or press the Cut button without a cutting mat in place and without a design and cartridge ready to go. Select the STOP button if you've made a mistake during the cutting process, the blade will stop cutting and from there you can correct your mistake. The Off button turns the machine off.

Roller Bar

The roller bar piece of the Cricut Cutter machine has wheels called star wheels. Star wheels allow materials to not shift when cutting. However, when cutting thick materials like felt and foam the star wheels can leave marks and indents in the material. To avoid this marking from the star wheels moves the star wheels all the way to the right side of the rubber bar one by one. If the cartridge is in the way of this maneuver turn your Cricut Cutter Machine off by selecting the OFF button and gently move the cartridge over to either side. To make sure that the material still is not passed over by the star wheels make sure the material has at least one inch away from the right side of the rubber bar where the star wheels are now located.

Display Screen

The display screen on your Cricut Cutter machine shows the design in which the machine will be cutting. The design can be edited on the display screen. Settings for your Cricut machine are also accessible through the display screen, such as: calibrating the screen and resetting the machine. A few common problems with the Display Screen include the LCD being unresponsive, the screen stuck on the End User License Agreement, the display screen being pixelated, and the screen stuck on the Tap to Zoom message. If you have any of these issues turn your machine off, then perform a hard reset. It is important to take care of your Display Screen as it is a vital part of your Cricut Cutter machine.

Do I need all these tools?

While these tools are all great in helping you create a project, you will be glad to know that you do not need to have every single tool mentioned above to use a Cricut effectively. However, among the must-have items are the mat and the tools mentioned in the Essential Tool Set. These are extremely helpful to complete your projects especially the ones with tiny cuts. A good way to begin your Cricut crafting journey is to equip yourself with the basics, such as the mat, the Tweezer, and the Weeder to start off and then slowly add on other items.

Where do I get these supplies?

One of the best ways to score a good deal with Cricut supplies that are good quality and the right ones is directly from Cricut. By signing up for their emails, you will be informed of any sale or discounts that Cricut has all the time. You can also go online and look out for crafters' blogs and craft sites that use Cricut, and you'll find codes that you can use to get 10% discounts on your purchases. Not only that, you can get free shipping. You can also check out your local craft store to see if there are any items at the clearance unit. Do take note though that some codes offered by crafts stores may not be applicable on the Cricut online store.

Another good place to purchase discounted or cheap Cricut supplies is on Amazon and even eBay.

Start Using Your Cricut Machine

How to Set Up Your Cricut Machine

There are different platforms you can use to set up your Cricut machine including Windows/Mac and iOS/Android platforms. I will briefly explain the steps for setting up your Cricut machine using any of the platforms, depending on the one available to you:

For Windows/Mac:

1. Use the power outlet to plug your Cricut machine.

2. Power ON your Cricut machine

3. Use the USB cable to connect your computer and your Cricut machine. Alternatively, connect via Bluetooth

4. Go to your internet browser and open it

5. Navigate to design.Cricut.com/setup

6. Follow to instruction on your screen to create your Cricut ID or sign in if you already have one.

7. Download the Design Space plugin when you are requested to do so.

8. Install the Design Space to your computer. To download the Design Space plugin and install it is super simple. To know that your setup process is complete is when you are prompted to start your first project.

For iOS/Android

1. Use the power outlet to plug your Cricut machine.

2. Power ON your Cricut machine

3. Pair your Cricut machine with your iOS or Android device via Bluetooth

4. Download the Design Space plugin and install it.

5. Launch the downloaded app

6. Create a Cricut ID to sign in and if you have one already, use it to sign in

7. Select the menu and tap Machine Setup & App Overview

8. Tap New Machine Setup

9. Follow the prompts on your screen to finish the setup

10. Again, to know that your setup process is complete is when you are prompted to start your first project.

Note that your machine is registered automatically during the setup process of your Cricut machine. There is no cause for alarm if, for any reason, you did not complete the process when you first connect your computer to your Cricut machine. Go to step 5 and continue from there using the on-screen instructions.

How to design with Cricut machine

I know that you have lot of ideas stuck in your brain and looking for a way to express them. What you need to do is set up your Cricut Explore Air machine, set up the Design Space, and start expressing those ideas immediately.

Working with Fonts in the Design Space

One of the unique features of the Cricut Design Space is the ability to brand your project with distinct fonts and text. Most project with Cricut machines start with the Design Space and you know what? There is more to it than meet the eye. Let me start with fonts in the Design Space.

How to Add Text to Cricut Design Space

1. For users of Windows, navigate to the left-hand side of the Canvas and select the Text tool. For iOS or Android user, the Text tool is at the bottom-left of the screen.

2. Select the font size and the font type you wish to use and then type your text in the text box. Do not freak out when you did not choose the font parameters before typing the text, with Cricut Design Space, you can type the text before selecting the font on Windows/Mac computer.

3. Click or tap on any space outside the text box to close it.

How to Edit Text in Cricut Design Space

To edit the text is super simple. Double click on the text to show available options. Select the action you wish from the list of the options displayed including font style, type, size, letter and line spacing.

How to Edit Fonts

1. Select the text you wish to edit on the Canvas or you can insert text from design panel, or select a text layer from the Layers Panel.

2. When the Text Edit Bar pops up, you can start changing the font using the available options. These options include Font, Font Drop-Down, Font Filter, Style, Font Size, Line Space, Alignment, and more.

How to Write Using Fonts

A simple way to write font using Cricut pen with Cricut Explore Air machine is to change the line type of your text from 'Cut' to 'Write'. Next is to choose the font type you wish to use and select the "Writing style" of your choice. Note that the fonts used in the Writing style is similar to the text written by hand but the Cricut machine will write it as if it is tracing the outside of the letters. I believe you know how to use fonts now and what the final form of the fonts will look like. Now, I want to discuss the different types of fonts.

System Fonts

System fonts refer to fonts installed on your computer or mobile device. Every time you sign in, the Cricut Design Space will automatically access your system fonts and allow you to use them for free in the Design Space projects.

Some system fonts have design components that are not compatible with Cricut Design space because they were not designed by Cricut. Do not be surprise when you encounter failure to import them into the Design Space, or they behave unusual while using them in the Design Space. Use the instructions on the font site or app when downloading fonts to your device or computer.

How to Use Images in Cricut Design Space

The Cricut library has more than 50,000 images and these images are updated from time to time. The Cricut Design space permits you to use some of these images for free in order to find out if these images fit into your desired project before buying them. You can also upload your personally designed image unto the canvas. Here are simple steps on how to use image(s) in your project:

1. Sign in to your Design Space and create a new project

2. Tap on Image button in the bottom left corner of your screen if you are using iOS/Android device or click on Images at the left-hand side of your screen if you are using Windows/Mac computer.

3. Browse the images to choose the ones you wish to use in your project. Use any of the options below:

- All Images—use this to search for a particular image in your Library or view featured images.

- Categories—use this to browse images by selecting the image categories.
- Cartridges—use this to search through the alphabetical list of more than 400 Cricut cartridges or even search for a specific one.

4. Insert your desired image(s) into your project and start editing them.

How to Cut One Image out of Another Image

It is possible to remove a part of an image to form another image using the Slice tool in Design Space and is super easy too. Use these steps to remove an image out of another image:

1. Position the two images to overlap each other.

2. Select the two images.

3. Click on "Slice". This button is at the bottom of the Layers Panel for computer users, in the Actions' menu at the bottom of the screen for Android and iOS users.

4. Separate the layers to check your new shapes.

5. Edit or delete the images separately.

6. Go to Layer and slice your image till you get your desired design.

How to Upload Images on Cricut Design Space

There are two types of images that you can upload to the Design Space which are Basic and Vector images. Basic images include file type like .jpg, .gif, .bmp, and .png while Vector images include files such as .svg and .dxf.

Here are the step by step instructions on how to upload images on Design Space via different platforms:

On Windows/Mac

1. Select Upload on the design panel on the left-hand side of the Canvas.

2. Use the Browse button to find your desired image from the computer or drag and drop the file to the upload window.

3. To upload Basic images, use these steps:

- Select your desired basic image file, select Open or drag and drop the file unto the Design Space
- Describe your image on the screen as either simple, moderately complex or complex
- Select Continue
- Define the cut lines of your image by editing unwanted background.

- Select the Preview to view the cut lines of your image. If you are satisfied with the image, select Continue.
- Name your image and tag it. Also decide how you intend to save it, either as Cut or Print and Cut image. Note that saving your image as Print Then Cut will save the entire image.
- Select Save when you are done.

4. If on the other hand, you intend to upload Vector image, then use these steps:

- Select the Vector image file you wish to upload then select Open or use drag and drop the file unto the Design Space.
- Name your image and tag it as stated in Basic image option.
- Click the image and select insert images to include it on your design screen.

On iOS device:

1. Tap the Upload tool at the bottom toolbar.

2. Choose Browse files to search the image you intend to upload from the available storage applications on your device.

3. If it is Basic image, clean the image and define the cut lines of the image. You can use these options:

- Remove-this will remove connected areas having the same color.
- Erase- Use this option to remove unwanted areas of the image you wish to eliminate.
- Crop- use this option to trim the edges of your image.

4. After cleaning your image, select Next at the upper right corner of your screen

5. Make final adjustments at your image before you save it your library.

6. Tap Next

7. Name your final image and save it either as Cut image or Print Then Save.

8. Click Save at the upper right corner of your screen.

9. Select the image to insert unto the Canvas from the Uploaded images library.

On Android device:

1. Tap the Upload button at the bottom panel

2. Choose to take a photo, choose from the photo library or open uploaded images

3. Select the file storage application where your image is located

4. For Vector images, enter the name and tap "Save".

5. For Basic images, use the options Remove, Erase and Crop to modify your image.

6. Click Done when you have finished cleaning the image.

7. Tap Next at the upper right corner of the screen.

8. Name your image and choose how to save it.

9. Select the image you wish to upload unto the Canvas.

Making Your First Project Ideas

Now that you have all of your goodies, what happens next? You might feel a little overwhelmed by the endless possibilities and wonder what you can do afterward. I stared at my Cricut Maker for two whole days, contemplating whether I should dare to start a project or not. My mother, being the curious cat that she is, used my own machine before me because I didn't want to mess anything up. I had her set it up, learn how to work the unit, and then show me what to do. You might think it was silly, but to me, it wasn't. I neither want to become disappointed nor break or mess with any of the settings. It's not as if that is actually that easy to do, but I still had that fear. It was the most expensive thing I had bought for myself in a very long time so the moment was big. The fact that my mother was figuring it out before me pulled me out of that hole, and I realized that if she could do it - the squinting, index finger typer – then it was possible for me too. After that day, I learned everything else myself and discovered that it's really so simple. I still feel silly about being so scared about the instructions that happen to be as clear as day. I am grateful that I had someone to kick me into a start, although you don't need someone to show you how or force you to do that because all you have to do is follow the guidelines. All of your answers will be answered shortly.

In your box, you will find everything you need to do your first project. This is very cute to me. It does not matter if you didn't purchase additional tools or materials because the basics are there, and you can give the machine a go! It really is a very considerate thing to add to the box, and I am truly happy about that. Many people would have forgotten to buy supplies because they are so excited for their Cricut. And since it is your first practice project, if you mess up, you won't be ruining those pretty materials that you have already purchased.

After setting up your Cricut machine according to the instruction, there will be directions on your screen that you must follow to create your first project.You will still be using the link you found on the paper when you were setting up your machine. If you have not yet received your machine and are interested in knowing how it works, or you are looking for extra clarifications, here's what it will say.

<u>First Step</u>

First off, load a pen into the accessories clamp. You can pick whichever color you think will go best with the paper you have received. Next, you want to turn the knob so that the indicator is pointed to "cardstock", considering that is what you will be working with. Have you had a proper look at your mats yet? The blue mat is what you will want to use for this project. You should remove the plastic cover - keep it, don't throw it away as you will need to re-cover your mat when you're done to avoid dust accumulation - and lay down the paper on the mat with the top left corners of the material and the grid aligned.

Second Step

Make sure that the paper is pressed flat before you push it between the rollers firmly. The mat has to rest on the bottom roller. When it is in place, press the "Load" button to load your mat between the rollers. Press the "go" button, which will be flashing at this stage, and wait for the machine to work its magic on your project. It's really cool to watch this process unfold. Once everything is done, the light will flash, and you can press the "Load" button again to unload the mat. Your paper will still be sticking to the mat when you remove it.

Third Step

Be careful when removing the material from the mat. Don't be too hasty; take your time so that it doesn't tear. Pull the mat away from the cardstock instead of doing it the other way around. After completing that step, you can now fold the cardstock in half, insert the liners into the corner slots of the card, and it's done!

You're Done!

You have just made your first ever Cricut project in a matter of minutes from start to finish! Congratulations! What are you waiting for? Go make more projects! There are a ton of templates you can play around with. Practice, practice, practice.

Personalized Ideas, Accessories and Stickers

As you become more familiar with your Cricut machine you will become more creative, and you will soon find yourself coming up with new project ideas all day long. The Cricut website and Design Space are both great tools for project ideas to help get you started if you are not sure what type of project you would like to begin. Pinterest is also another great online resource for project ideas at different levels of difficulty.

Always keep in mind when starting a new project that you first must have all of the materials necessary to complete the project. It is always helpful to check your stock of tools and materials before getting started. The worst feeling is when you sit down and begin working on a difficult project only to realize you are out of a specific material needed to finish the job. It will save you a lot of time in the long run if you spend a few minutes at the beginning taking stock of your inventory! Working with materials you already have on hand is also a great way to keep your crafting costs low. It will always feel good to know that you made a custom piece of work without spending a ton of extra money just to complete it!

Vinyl

Creative Custom Vinyl Candles

Supplies Needed:

- Cricut Essential Tool Set

- Cutting Mat

- Transfer Tape

Step One: Pick your Quote and Design it in Design Space

Be sure to select a font that is easy to read. There are many different quote options already predesigned in Design space that you will have immediate access to. You will also have access to quite a few more design ideas for free if you are a Cricut Access Member. Here you can change the font size, color, and script. Once you have your design just as you want it, you can move on to the next step!

<u>Step Two: Measure, Cut and Place Vinyl on your Mat</u>

You will want to start this project by selecting the type of vinyl you want to use, in this project I would recommend permanent vinyl. You will then want to grab your 12"x12" mat with either standard or light grip. This type of mat usually works best with vinyl material. You will want to line up the vinyl to the grid on the cutting mat. This grid lines up with the grid in design space (if you choose to have the grid showing while you design). This will help you minimize waste as you can cut off only the exact amount of material you need to complete this project.

<u>Step Three: Cut Out Vinyl</u>

Before cutting, ensure that your Cricut machine is set to the right setting to cut vinyl. You can select a thin vinyl setting or set the cut to a thicker level, just to ensure that the Cricut machine cuts all the way through the vinyl on the first go round. You will want to back to stay intact, however (this will make weeding a lot easier when you get to this in the next stop) so don't overdo the cut pressure. Once you are secure in your vinyl placement on the mat, as well as your machine setting you are ready to go! Once the mat is loaded and the cut button on your Cricut Machine is blinking, you are ready to hit the button and begin cutting.

Design Space will give you a percentage as to how far into the project it has cut.

Step Four: Remove Vinyl from Mat and Begin Weeding

This step is where you will need your trusty Cricut Weeder! You will want to remove all of the excess vinyl away from the cut that you want to put on your candle. Weeding can be tedious, and you will either end up loving it or hate it! This part of the project will also take some time depending on how difficult a design you choose. This is also a great step in a project to use your Cricut Bright pad if you have one. This will help illuminate the cut lines and help you differentiate between the excess vinyl and the pieces you want to keep. A wise investment if you truly enjoy intricate cut pieces with lots of weeding!

Step Five: Apply Transfer Tape

Transfer Tape is the material that will allow you to remove your vinyl design from its original backing and place it onto your project surface. The transfer tape will attach to the front of the vinyl, which is not sticky, and pull it from its original backing to expose the sticky side of the vinyl. You will want to ensure your design is fully stuck to the transfer tape before trying to remove it from the original backing. It is strongly recommended to smooth the transfer tape over your original design using your

Cricut Scraper. This will also help you remove any air bubbles that may develop during the transfer tape applied to your design. Once you feel your design is securely stuck to the transfer tape, begin removing the design from the original backing.

Step Six: Apply Vinyl to Project Surface

Once your design is removed from the original backing you are ready to apply the design to your project surface via the transfer tape. You will want to follow the same process of smoothing the design onto the surface with your Cricut scraper and removing all of the air bubbles that will likely develop because the surface of a candle is typically curved. Transfer tape is usually fairly forgiving if you need to remove the design and reposition it before starting over. Once you feel your design is full stuck onto the project surface, you can begin to slowly remove the transfer tape. It should easily come off of the design, while the design continues to stick to the project surface. If you find that the transfer tape is pulling the design off of the project surface, stop and smooth the design back onto the project surface again with your scraper. You may have to do this a few times before the vinyl will stick. Once you have the vinyl fully stuck with the transfer tape removed, your project is complete!

You will follow a similar guideline for any type of vinyl project you may choose. There will always be adjustments depending on the type of vinyl you are using and the difficulty of the cut. Ultimately if you follow this step by step guide you will easily be creating multiple vinyl projects. Similar vinyl projects include coasters, drink cups, and car window monograms. This sample project is a great way to get started in the vinyl world.

Leather

Leather Pouch

Supplies Needed:

- Cricut Brand Genuine Leather

- X-actor knife or rotary cutter

- Deep Cut Blade

- Cricut Strong grip cutting mat

- Scoring Tool

- Heavy Duty Snaps

- Fabric Adhesive

Step One: Set Up Your Machine and Leather on the strong grip cutting mat

The first thing you will need to do is load up your machine with the genuine leather already pressed into a strong grip mat. This will ensure that the leather will not bump into the black bumper as it feeds into the machine. You will also want to cut down the right edge of the piece of genuine leather as it only needs to be 11 inches wide. Then you will want to move the four-star wheels or the little white wheels on your Cricut machine, over to the right so that you can run the material without bumping the wheels. Next and most importantly you will want to load your deep cut blade before starting this project.

Step Two: Loading the design pattern into Design Space

There is a premade design ready to go with Cricut Access in Design Space. The best thing about Cricut Access premade designs is that all you have to do is hit "make it" and it will load all of the materials settings, there is no need to size it! Select your machine and material. Note: If you are using the Cricut Explore make sure you have the dial turned to Custom in order to get all these options. This is where you will want to load your scoring tool to the accessories slot as well.

Step Three: Hit "Go" and watch the Cricut machine to make magic!

It is also recommended to go a test piece before running an entire sheet of leather into the machine. Similar to measure first cut once, always run a test design with scraps left over from prior projects!

Step Four: Add Snaps and Glue in Flaps

You will want to follow the directions on your snap kit to learn how to properly install the snaps on your leather pouch. You will want to glue the flaps in last so that you can ensure it lines up with the snaps secured.

The leather project above gives you a great opportunity to take advantage of the predesigned projects that are readily available with Cricut Access in Design Space. This one does require more technical advantages and has a higher degree of difficulty over the vinyl project also recommended. Safety always comes first, and it is recommended you read through the entire instructions to a project such as this before beginning the project yourself. It is also a good idea to have a helper on hand in the event you will need another pair of hands. Once you have a few practices rounds under your belt you should feel more comfortable doing this project on your own.

We sincerely hope you enjoy these sample projects we have provided for you. These are just two samples of what your new Cricut machine is capable of making. Anything you can dream up is an option for you to make on your Cricut machine, and this probably why the machine has gotten so popular in recent years! Feel free to begin your Cricut journey with these projects and others that are free for Cricut users all over the internet. Always remember that Cricut access is also a great resource for finding premade and designed projects ready to go!

Complex Operations

Cricut machines are pretty straightforward with what you need to do in order to make simple designs, but you might wonder about some of the more complex operations. Here, we'll tell you how to accomplish these with just a few simple button presses.

Blade Navigation And Calibration

The blades that come with a Cricut machine are important to understand, and you will need to calibrate your blades every single time you use your machine.

Each blade needs this because it will help you figure out which level of depth and pressure your cut needs to be. Typically, each blade needs to be calibrated only once, which is great, because then you don't have to spend time doing this each time. Once you've done it once, it will stay calibrated, but if you decide to change the housings of the blades or if you use them in another machine, you'll need to calibrate it again.

So, if you plan on using a knife blade and then a rotary blade, you'll want to make sure that you do recalibrate – and make sure you do this before you start with your project. It is actually incredibly easy to do this though, which is why it's encouraged.

To calibrate a blade, you just launch the Design Space, and from there, you open the menu and choose calibration. Then, choose the blade that you're going to put in. For the purpose of this explanation, let's say you're using a knife blade.

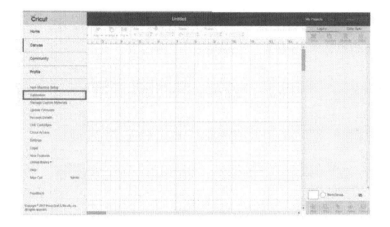

Put that blade in the clamp B area and do a test cut, such as with copy paper into the mat, and then load that into the machine.

Press continue, then press the go button on the machine. It will then do everything that you need for the item itself, and it will start to cut.

You can then choose which calibration is best for your blade, but usually, the first one is good enough.

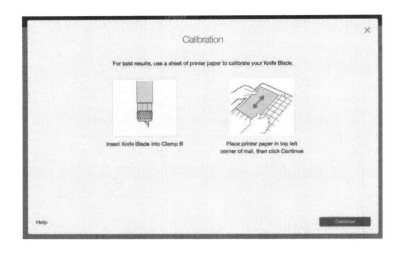

You can do this with every blade you use, and every time you use a new blade on your machine, I highly recommend you do this – for best results, of course.

Set Paper Size

Setting paper size in a Cricut machine is actually pretty simple. You will want to use this with either cartridge or with Design Space for what you'd like to make. This also comes with a cutting mat, and you'll want to load this up with paper so that you can use it.

To do this, you'll want to make sure that you have it plugged in, then go to the project preview screen. If you choose a material that's bigger than the mat size, it will automatically be changed, and it'll be adjusted as necessary based on the size of the material that you select.

You can choose the color, the size of the material, whether or not it'll mirror – and you can also choose to fully skip the mat, too, if you don't want that image printed just yet.

Note that the material size menu does offer sizes that are bigger than the largest mat available.

If you're planning on using the print then cut mode, do understand that it's limited to a print area of 8.5x11 inches, but again, you can choose these settings for yourself.

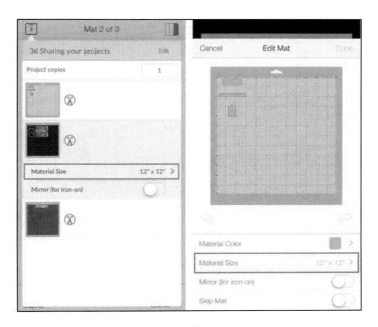

Load Last

To load that paper and image last is pretty simple. Remember that "skip this mat" step? Literally, press that, and then go. You'll be able to skip this quite easily. It's one of those operations that's definitely a little different from what you may be used to, but if you want to skip design and don't want to work with it just yet, this is probably the best option for you to use. If you're worried about forgetting it, don't worry – Cricut will remind you.

Paper Saver

Saving paper is something you'll want to consider doing with a Cricut machine because it loves to eat up the paper before you even start decorating. The Explore Air 2 definitely will appreciate it if you save paper, and there are a few ways to do so.

The first one is, of course, to halve your mats. But you don't need to do only that.

You can also go to the material saver option on the machine, which will automatically adjust and align your paper as best it can. Unfortunately, on newer machines, it's actually not directly stated, but there is a way to save paper on these.

You'll want to create tabbed dividers to organize your projects and save them directly there.

The first step is to create a background shape. Make sure that the paper looks like a background. Go to shapes, and then select the square to make the square shape.

Next, once you've created squares to represent the paper, arrange this to move to the back so that the shapes are organized to save the most space on each mat. Then organize the items that are on top of where the background is and arrange them so they all fit on a singular mat.

Rotating is your best friend – you can use this feature whenever you choose objects, so I do suggest getting familiarized with it.

Next, you hide the background at this point, and you do this by choosing the square, and in Design Space, literally hiding this on the right side. Look at the eyeball on the screen, and you'll see a line through the eyeball. That means it's hidden.

Check over everything and fine-tune it at this point. Make sure they're grouped around one object, and make sure everything has measurements. Move these around if they're outside of the measurements required.

Once they're confirmed, you then attach these together on the right-hand side of Design Space, which keeps everything neatly together – they're all cut from the same sheet.

From here, repeat this until everything is neatly attached. It will save your paper, but will it save you time? That's debatable, of course.

Speed Dial

So, the speed dial typically comes into play when you're setting the pressure and speed. Fast mode is one of the options available on the Explore Air 2 and the Maker machines, which make the machine run considerably faster than other models. You can use this with vinyl, cardstock, and iron-on materials. To set this, go to the cut screen. You'll have a lot of speed dials here, and various different settings. If you have the right material in place when choosing it, you'll be given the option to do it quickly with fast mode. From there, you simply tap or click on that switch in order to toggle this to the position for on. That will activate fast mode for that item.

It will make everything about two times faster, which means that if you're making complex swirl designs, it will take 30 seconds instead of the 73-second average it usually takes.

However, one downside to this is that because it's so fast, it will sometimes make the cuts less precise – you'll want to move back to the regular mode for finer work.

This is all usually set with the smart-set dial, which will offer the right settings for you to get the best cuts that you can on any material you're using. Essentially, this dial eliminates you having to manually check the pressure on this.

To change the speed and pressure for a particular material that isn't already determined with the preset settings, you will need to select custom mode and choose what you want to create. Of course, the smart-set dial is better for the Cricut products and mats. If you notice that the blade is cutting too deep or not deep enough, there is a half-settings option on each material that you can adjust to achieve the ideal cut.

Usually, the way you do this with the pre-set settings is to upload and create a project, press go, and load the mat, then move the smart-set dial on the machine itself to any setting. Let's select custom and choose the speed for this one.

In Design Space, you then choose the material, add the custom speed, and you can adjust these settings. You can even adjust the number of times you want the cut to be changed with the smart-set dial, too. Speed is something you can adjust to suit the material, which can be helpful if you're struggling with putting together some good settings for your items.

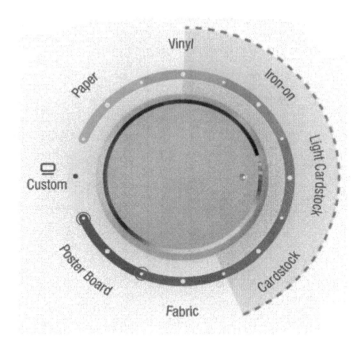

Vinyl

Paper

Iron-on

Light Cardstock

Custom

Poster Board

Cardstock

Fabric

Pressure Dial

Now, let's talk about pressure. Each piece of material will require different pressure settings. If you're not using enough pressure, the blade won't cut into the material, and if you use too much pressure, you'll end up cutting the mat, which isn't what you want to do.

The smart-set dial kind of takes the guesswork out of it. You simply choose the setting that best fits your material, and from there, you let it cut. If you notice you're not getting a deep enough cut, then you'll want to adjust it about half a setting to get a better result. From there, adjust as needed.

But did you know that you can change the pressure on the smart-set dial for custom materials? Let's say you're cutting something that's very different, such as foil, and you want to set the pressure to be incredibly light so that the foil doesn't get shredded. What you do is you load the material in, and you choose the custom setting. You can then choose the material you plan to cut, such as foil – and if it's not on the list, you can add it.

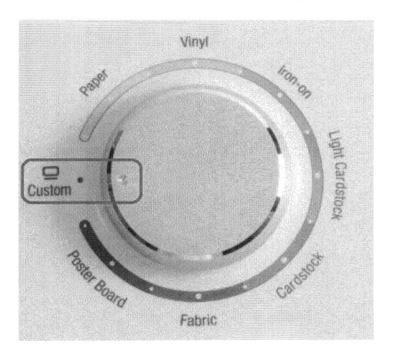

From here, you're given pressure options. Often, people will go too heavy with their custom settings, so I do suggest that you go lighter for the first time and change it as needed. There is a number of draggers that goes from low to high. If you need lots of pressure, obviously let it go higher. If you don't need much pressure, make sure it's left lower. You will also want to adjust the number of times the cut is done on a multi-cut feature item.

This is a way for you to achieve multiple cuts for the item, which can be incredibly helpful for those who are trying to get the right cut, or if the material is incredibly hard to cut. I don't suggest using this for very flimsy and thin material, because it'll just waste your blade and the mat itself.

That's all there is to it! This is a great way to improve on your Cricut designs. Personally, I love to work with custom cuts, and you can always delete these if you feel like they don't work. You just press the change settings button to adjust your pressure, speed, or how many cuts you want, and then choose to save when you're done.

What if you don't like a setting, period? You can delete it, of course!

To delete, go to materials settings, and you'll see a little trash can next to it. Press the trash can, and the setting will be removed.

Adjusting the pressure and cuts is part of why people love using Design Space, and it's a great feature to try.

Cricut Design Space

Design Space lets you do many things with your Cricut machine. Here are a few things you can do with this convenient app:

● Aligning various items right next to one another.

● Attaching items to hold images in place, and lets you use score lines.

● Arranging these to make them sit on the canvas in different layers.

● Canvas, a tool that lets you arrange prints and vectors so you can use the various tools with them.

● Contouring, which is a tool that lets you hide image layers quickly, so they're not cut out.

● Color sync, which lets you use multiple colors in one project to reduce the material differences.

● Cut buttons, which will start cuts.

● Make it button: this is the screen that lets you see the designs being cut.

- Draw lines: lets you draw with the pen to write images and such.

- Fill: lets you fill in a pattern or color on an item.

- Flipping items flip it horizontally or vertically by 180 degrees.

- Group: puts different text and images on a singular layer, and everything is moved at once so that it doesn't affect the layout.

- Linetype: an option that you can do with your piece, whether you want to cut a line, draw a line, or score a line.

- Mirrored image: reverses it, which is very important with transfer vinyl, so everything reads correctly.

- Print then Cut: it's an option that lets you print the design, and from there, the machine cuts it.

- Redo: does an action again and reverses it.

- Reverse Weeding: removes the vinyl that's left behind, and it's used mostly for stencil vinyl

- Score lines: helps you make creases in the papers so you can fold it.

- SVG: this is a scalable vector graphic that lets you cut a file that's scaled to be larger or smaller so that the resolution is kept, and made up of lines that consist of infinite white dots.

- Texts and fonts: let you use put specialized fonts and words within Design Space.

- Weeding: lets you remove the excess vinyl from designs. Press this when you're cutting vinyl.

- Welding: a tool you use when you want to combine two line shapes into one shape, and it's used to make seamless cursive words.

These are most of the functions you can do in Design Space. To use these, simply choose an image or font that you want to use and put it in Design Space. From there, you can do literally whatever you need to do with it – within reason, of course – and then put the image onto the material that you're using. For the purposes of learning, I suggest not getting in too deep with vinyl just yet, and get used to using these tools. You also have pens, which can be implemented to help you write images with a tool that looks sharp and crisp.

Cricut Pens

Pens for your Cricut machine are essentially another way to get creative with your projects. I love to use them for cards, handmade tags for gifts, or even fancy invites and labels.

Now, each pen offers a little different finish and point size. They aren't toxic, and they are permanent once they're dried. You've got the extra-fine points for small lettering, up to a medium tip for making thicker lines. There are also glitter and metallic pens, so you have a lot of options to choose from!

But do you have to use them? Well, the answer is no. You can use different pens, but test them on paper first and get adapters to use with them. Cricut pens are your best option.

To use these, choose the wording or design, or whatever you want to do. You want to go to the layers panel that's on the right-hand side, and choose the scissors icon – change that to the write icon. From there, you'll want to choose the pen color that you would like to use.

You can then have the design printed out on the material you're using.

Some people like to use different fonts, whether it be system fonts or Cricut fonts, or the Cricut Access fonts. However, the one thing with Design Space is that it will write what will normally be cut, so you'll get an outline of that font rather than just a solid stroke of writing.

This can add to the design, however – you essentially change the machine from cut to write, and there you go.

You can also use the Cricut writing fonts, which you can choose by going to a blank canvas, and then choosing the text tool on the left-hand side, along with the wording you'd like for this to have.

Once you're in the font edit toolbar, you are given a font selection. You choose the writing font filter, so you have fonts that you can write with. From there, choose the font, and then switch from the scissors to the pen icon, and then select the pen color. That's all there is to it!

You can also use this with Cricut Access – if you're planning on using this a lot, it might be worth it.

To insert the pens into the Cricut machine, you want to choose to make it, and from there, you'll then go to the prepare mat screen. It will say draw instead of writing in the thumbnail this time around, so you press continue in the bottom right-hand corner, then put the pen into clamp A – you just unlock it and then put it in. Wait until it clicks, and that's it!

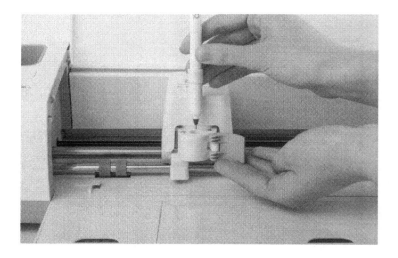

Cricut pens are super easy, and it's a great idea to consider trying these out.

As you can see, there are many different Cricut features and a lot of functions that may seem complex, but as you can see are really not that hard. There are tons of options for your Cricut projects, and a lot that you can get out of this machine.

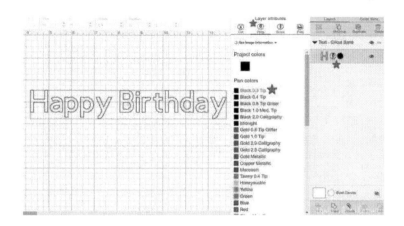

Maintenance Of Cricut Machine

Every Cricut machine needs to be cleaned and taken care of in order to keep it working for as long as possible.

Here, you'll learn about the maintenance required for Cricut machines, and what you can do to keep your machine working efficiently.

<u>Cleaning and Care</u>

Cleaning your machine is very important, and you should do it regularly to keep everything in tip-top shape.

If you don't take care of your machine, that's just money down the drain. But what can you do to care for your machine?

Well, I do suggest initially that you make sure to run maintenance on it as much as you can and keep it clean.

There are a few other tips and tricks that can help prolong the machine's life. For starters, keep liquids and food away from the machine – never drink or eat while you use your Cricut machine.

Set up your machine in a location that's free of dust and try to keep it away from excessive coolness or heat, so don't just throw it in the attic or an especially cold basement.

If you're transporting your machine to use it at a different location, never leave it in the car.

Excessive heat will melt the machine's plastic components, so be careful.

Finally, make sure the machine is stored away from sunlight. Keep it out of places in the home where sunlight hits it directly.

For example, if you have an office that is very bright and the sun warms the machine for a long period of time, you'll want to move it so that it doesn't get damaged.

Be gentle with your machine. Remember, it is a machine, so you'll want to make sure that you do take some time and try to keep it nice and in order.

Don't be rough with it, and when working with the machine parts, don't be too rough with them, either.

Caring for your machine isn't just about making sure that the parts don't get dirty, but you should also make sure that you keep everything in good working order.

Cleaning the Machine Itself

In general, the exterior is pretty easy to clean – you just need a damp cloth. Use a soft cloth to wipe it off, and keep in mind that chemical cleaners with benzene, acetone, or carbon tetrachloride should never be used on your Cri-cut machine.

Any cleaner that is scratchy, as well, should be avoided at all costs. Make sure that you never put any machine components in water.

This should be obvious, but often, people may use a piece of a damp cloth, thinking that it'll be fine when in reality, it isn't.

You should consider getting some non-alcoholic wipes for cleaning your machine.

Always disconnect the power before cleaning, as you would with any machine.

The Cricut machine can then be lightly wiped down. Some people also use a glass cleaner sprayed on a cloth but do be careful to make sure no residue builds up.

If you notice there is some dust there, you can typically get away with a cloth that's soft and clean.

Sometimes, grease can build up – you may notice this on the cartridge bar if you use cartridges a lot.

Use a swab of cotton or a soft cloth to remove it.

Greasing the Machine

If you need to grease your machine, first make sure that it's turned off and the smart carriage is moved to the left.

Use a tissue to wipe this down, and then move it to the right, repeating the process again.

From there, move the carriage to the center and open up a lubrication package.

Put a small amount onto a Q-tip.

Apply a thin coating, greasing everything evenly, and also clean any buildup that may have occurred.

This is usually the issue if you hear grinding noise when cleaning the machine itself.

There are a few other important places that you should make sure to clean, besides the outside and the carriage.

Any places where blades are should be cleaned; you can just move the housing unit of the blade to clean it.

You should also check the drawing area, to make sure there isn't any excessive ink there.

Never use spray cleaner directly on the machine, for obvious reasons.

The bar holding the housing shouldn't be wiped down, but if you do notice an excessive grease, please take the time to make sure that it's cleaned up.

Remember to never touch the gear chain near the back of this unit, either, and never clean with the machine on, for your own safety.

When caring for a Cricut machine, try to do this more frequently if you're using the machine a lot, or twice yearly.

If you notice strange noises coming from the machine, do get a grease packet. You can always contact Cricut and they'll help you figure out the issue, if there is one, with your machine.

Cricut machines are great, but you need to take care in making sure that you keep everything in rightful order.

<u>Cutting Blade</u>

Your blades will tend to dull over time, but this is usually a very slow process.

The best way to prevent it is to have different blades to cut different materials.

Having a different blade for each material is a really good idea. You can get

fine-point ones which are good for smaller items; deep-cut, which is great for leather and other fabrics; bonded fabric, so great for fabric pieces; a rotary blade for those heavy fabrics; and finally, a knife blade, which is good for those really thick items.

In order to maintain your blades, you should clean the housing area for every blade after each use, since they get gunky fast.

Squirting compressed air into the area is a wonderful way to get the dust out of there.

As for the blades, remember foil? Use a little bit of that over the edges of the blade to help clean and polish them up.

To polish them, you should put them on the cutting mat and from there, cut small designs on it.

It actually does help with sharpening them, and it doesn't require you to completely remove them.

You can do this with every single blade, too!

To change the blades in their housings, just open the clamps, pull up, and remove the housing within the machine.

Put a new blade in, and then close it.

That's all it takes. Storing them is also pretty simple.

There is a drop-down doorway at the front area of the machine. It's made for storing the blades within their housings.

Put your loose blades in there first, then utilize the magnet to keep them in place.

The best part about this storage is that your blades are always with the Cricut, even if you take the machine somewhere else.

There is also a blade organizer that you can use, too, made out of chipboard with some holders attached. This is also a wonderful means to store all of your items.

Organizing your Cricut blades is very important, and understanding the best places to keep them is, of course, essential.

Cutting Mat

Your cutting mats need to be cleaned because if you don't clean them frequently, they will attract dirt and lose adhesiveness.

That means you'll have to spend more money on mats, which isn't ideal.

There are different ways to clean them, and we'll go over a few of the different means to clean your mats so you can use them for longer.

Cleaning the Mat Itself

First, if your mat is completely filthy, you need to clean it. Of course, you'll also want to do this for just general maintenance, too. Once it's been cleaned, you'll notice it's sticky again.

Typically, washing it down with either a magic eraser or a kitchen scrubber can do it.

Sometimes, if it's really dirty, you might want to get some rubbing alcohol onto a wipe.

If you notice a chunk of the debris left behind, however, is fabric oriented, hen get some lint rollers or even just stick some scotch tape on there and pull it off.

This can eliminate the issue.

But what about the really tough grime? Well, get some Goo Gone cleaner. Put a little bit on the troublesome spots and wipe it around, and then let the goo stick on there.

From there, get an old card or something to get it off, and then wash the mat. Once it's dry, check to see if it's sticky. If it is, then great – you don't need to do anything more.

But what if you notice that it's still not sticky? Well, why not restick the cutting mat itself!

Resticking The Mat

To do this, you need to make sure that you tape the edges, so you don't get adhesive near the edges, and mess with the rollers of the machine. Once that's there, use either spray adhesive or glue stick, and then let it dry.

If you notice that it's still not sticky enough when you're finished applying the first coat, apply a second coat.

There are great adhesives out there, such as simple spray adhesive, easy tack, quilt basting, bonding, and also repositionable e glue.

All of these are fairly effective, and if you notice that the mat is actually sticking pretty well, then you're in luck.

However, always make sure that you let this fully dry.

If you don't let the adhesive dry and you start using the mat again, you will run into the problem of the material being stuck to it.

Once it's dried, try it out with some test material.

If you find it too sticky at this point, but either your hands or a shirt on there to help reduce the tackiness.

Caring for Machines and Mats

Here are a couple of other tips to use with your cutting mats.

The first, use different mats. You may notice that you can get more out of one type of mat than another kind, which is something many people don't realize.

Often, if you notice that you get a lot more out of the firmer grip mats, buy more of those.

Finally, halve your mats.

You can save immensely by making sure that they're cut in half. This does work, and it helps pretty well. You can expect anywhere from about 25 to 40 different cuts before you'll need to replace the mat, but cleaning after about half of that can definitely help with improving the quality of your cuts.

The life of the mat, of course, does vary based on the settings and what materials you cut. When you can't get it to stick, try cleaning and resticking it, but if you notice that it's still not doing the job, you're going to need to get a replacement.

Taking care of your Cricut machine will get you more use out of it, so make sure you perform regular maintenance on all your machine's components so it can be used for years.

The Best Cricut Machine To Buy

Purchasing a Cricut Machine may not be very cheap, but choosing your model should mostly depend on your needs, and what you wish to do with these machines. If you have never used a Cricut machine before, then you will need to start with the easiest machine to operate. As a manufacturer of tools and accessories for DIY crafts, Cricut has several models that can serve all kinds of users. From all the Cricut Models, there are four which are most interesting: the ones from the Explore family (Cricut Explore One, Cricut Explore Air, and Cricut Explore Air 2), and of course, the Cricut Maker, which is the best Cricut Machine you can hope for.

Before you even start to think about the price of these models, it would be nice to understand what they can do.

Cricut Explore One

This machine is the most basic one you can get from the Explore family. Derived from its predecessor (Cricut Explore), this tool can be the perfect starter machine for you if you are not familiar with any of the Cricut products. Like most of the Cricut products, it's compatible with Design Space software (and allows you to upload your own images free of charge), can work with Cricut Cartridges, or can cut a pretty wide variety of materials. Plus, it comes with Smart Set Dial, a function you can use to easily configure the settings for each material.

If you just want to start your own small business, and have something pretty interesting in mind but you don't want to invest too much, for now, the Cricut Explore One can be the perfect choice for you. It can be bought for less than $200 on the Cricut website, Amazon, or other retailers. When you have great project ideas, then the sky is the limit when it comes to how much money you can make from your Cricut projects, so spending this amount can be considered a minor and very profitable investment on your part.

Cricut Explore Air

If you are looking for an amazing DIY value, look no further, as the Cricut Explore Air can be the perfect choice for you. In terms of features, this version is a bit more advanced than the original Cricut Explore. It includes the Smart Set Dial, a double tool holder for writing and one-click cutting, and it works with Design Space software (for Mac/iOS/Windows/Android). Obviously, you will be able to upload your own images free of charge, but the machine can also work with Cricut Cartridges and cut plenty of materials.

When it comes to connectivity, Cricut Explore Air comes with a Bluetooth option for wireless cutting. This type of connectivity can be very handy in plenty of cases but bear in mind that it might fail if the projects you are trying to create are quite big.

The manufacturer, Amazon, or other retailers can offer great deals on this machine, so don't be shocked if you can find this product at a heavily discounted price. When you think of what it can do, it's definitely worth it to pay a discounted price for Cricut Explore Air.

Cricut Explore Air 2

If you are looking for the best product from the Explore Family, then you will need to try Cricut Explore Air 2. This machine is like an upgraded version of Explore Air, and it's known for its time-saving performance. It has more features than the prior versions, and so far, it's been a very appreciated product by plenty of users. The biggest advantage of this version is that it comes with both Smart Set dial and Fast Mode. So you can easily go through material settings, plus you write and cut 2 times faster, hence its time-saving performance and increased productivity.

Plus, you will get all the existing features of the Explore Family products like:

- Bluetooth connectivity for wireless cutting

- Double tool holding for both writing and one-click cutting

- It allows you to upload your own images using the Design Space software

- It can cut plenty of materials

- It can work with Cricut Cartridges

Therefore, if you are looking for a powerful Cricut Machine that has plenty of features and can be a time-saver, then the Cricut Explore Air 2 is the perfect choice for you. When it comes to the price, this version is a bit more expensive compared to the prior versions, but it totally worth the investment, especially when you buy this product at a discounted price, or with a bundle (this option may include different accessories).

Cricut Maker

Without any doubt, the premium or the flagship machine of Cricut is the Maker. If you are looking to expand your craft business, then this is the right tool for you. The Cricut Maker has plenty of features, as you can see below:

- it has Bluetooth connectivity included, for wireless cutting

- it comes with a double tool holder for writing and one-click cutting

- it allows you to upload your images for free using the Design Space software

- you can cut even more materials compared to the prior versions

- it comes with Fast Mode included, so you can write or cut two times faster

- it has a special Rotary Blade for fabrics

- it includes a Knife Blade for thicker materials

- Simple and Double Scoring Wheel

- Adaptive Tool System, which is a feature for cutting hundreds of other materials

Just FYI, you can use the Fast Mode option from the Cricut Explore Air 2 and Maker to work with cardstock, iron-on, and vinyl.

One of the best things with the Cricut machines is that you can select the color that you like the most, so it's not like you are limited to one color (white or black). Therefore, for the Explore version, you can select between Green and Wild Orchid. The Explore One comes with more color options: Blue, Pink Poppy, Navy Bloom, Coral, or Grey. You will get different color options with Explore Air: Gold, Teal, Wild Orchid, Poppy, and Blue. By far, the Explore Air 2 has the most options you can select from including White Pearl (Martha Stewart), Wisteria, Sunflower, Sky, Rose, Raspberry, Persimmon, Periwinkle, Peacock, Mint, Merlot, Lilac, Gold, Ivory (Anna Griffin), Fuschi, Denim, Coral, Cobalt, Cherry Blossom, Boysenberry, Blue, and Black.

The Cricut Maker only comes with three color options: Rose, Blue, and Champagne. Some colors may be exclusive to specific retailers, so these colors may not be found in the manufacturer's online store.

Choosing the Right Cricut for You

There are several aspects you will need to consider when selecting the right Cricut Machine for you, like:

• your experience with these kinds of machines

• your budget

• what projects you want to create

• what materials you want to cut

When you don't have too much experience with such machines, and you are definitely not familiar with any of the Cricut Machines, then it's wise to choose an entry-level machine from the Explore family. Perhaps this is why they included these machines in the Explore family, as it lets you explore the functions and features of a Cricut Machine. Any of these machines can be considered teasers of the Cricut Maker, which can be easily considered the ultimate cutting machine. If you are a beginner but want to quickly learn and implement some of your great ideas into projects, then the Cricut Explore Air 2 can be considered the perfect option for you. You can easily find a color you prefer, plus you will find all kinds of deals from the Cricut Shop or online retailers, offering you the product at a good price.

However, if you are very familiar with these machines, and you want to cut even thicker materials, then you really need to get the Cricut Maker, especially if you have some projects in mind that can help you make plenty of money. Regardless of the version you select, in most cases the prices are reasonable and you can easily recover your initial investment in such a machine.

Solving The Most Common Problems When Using Cricut

Frequent Cricut Problems and Solutions

Now that you're familiar with Cricut models and the Cricut Design Space, there are some challenges that you might encounter while using your Cricut.

The problems that we will mention will also come with solutions that you can quickly put in place in your home.

Your Transfer Tape isn't working

Using a transfer tape can be complicated and difficult to use sometimes, but the most frustrating part of using it is when it is used on your project, but then, it doesn't come up.

This problem is usually common when working with glitter, vinyl, and even glitter vinyl. When your transfer tape seems not to be working, that's probably because you're using the wrong one.

Some rolls of vinyl, when purchased, come with their transfer tape, or they recommend one for you. But this isn't the same for every case.

For example, when working with some projects, the Standard transfer tape is ideal. This usually happens if you are making use of the standard vinyl.

But, for other types of vinyl, you should probably use the StrongGrip transfer tape made by Cricut.

If you're looking for something cheap and quick, you can use painter's tape or contact paper.

Your Material is Tearing

Different reasons cause this, but the main reason is probably because of your cutting mat. If your cutting mat isn't sticky enough, the material will keep on cutting.

There are many reasons why your mat might not be working right. It could be that you're using the wrong mat for your project or that the mat is old, and the stickiness has already weakened.

The blue Cricut mat is the Light Grip mat. This is good for materials that don't need a lot of stickiness to stay in a place, like paper.

The purple Cricut mat is the Strong Grip mat, which is ideal for those materials that slip around a lot and might get damaged. This includes leather and some types of fabric.

Then there's the green Cricut mat, which is the Standard Grip mat. It's for anything that's not too light and not too strong.

It's essential to use the right mat for your materials, or else, you'll waste a lot of your materials.

There are some other reasons why your materials might be tearing instead of cutting.

The blade

Most often than not, you might have trouble with your blade. When using a blade, two things can go wrong. First, the blade might just be old and in need of replacement. Second, the blade you're using is not suitable for the material that you're cutting.

It's better to use the fine point blade whenever possible, but when you need a heavy hand, you should use the deep cut blade. Try not to use the deep cut blade for a lot of materials, or they will tear.

The settings

If none of the aforementioned works, you should also check the Design Space settings. You might not be using the right cut settings for the material.

Also, if the image that you're trying to cut out is very complicated, the material might cut it wrong because of the settings. So, you should change your cut settings to the cardstock intricate design settings.

The type of material

If nothing else works, then it might be safe to conclude that the material cannot be cut by your Cricut machine. There are over a hundred materials that can work with Cricut, and so this is highly unlikely.

But, if you've exhausted all your options, then you can test your machine with paper. If it cuts appropriately, you will know that the material you're trying to cut is not compatible with Cricut.

Your Blade isn't Cutting Right

If your blade isn't cutting right through the material, then that might cause problems for your design. There are a few solutions to this.

The most common mistake that people make is when they don't push their blade in all the way. If your blade isn't cutting through the material, ensure you placed the blade right.

Also, ensure that your blade is clean. If there is debris around your blade, then your blade won't work correctly. If there is debris, then you can clean the blade using compressed air.

Lastly, it could be your Cricut cut settings. Before cutting, you should check out the settings to make sure that everything is in place. If you want to clarify if the problem is the material, you can test the settings out with a small part of the material that you want to cut.

With these solutions, your blade should work right. If not, then your blade isn't right for the material that you're cutting.

Problems with Images

The images aren't showing on the mat

The first and common problem with images is when they aren't showing on the mat. This happens when you have made a perfect design on Cricut Design Space, but when you cut it, you don't see your images.

If you have this problem, it's straightforward to fix it. Go to your design, click on 'Group,' and then 'Attach' from the layers panel. This will ensure that your designs stay where you placed them, and so when you cut, everything will be where they're supposed to be.

Converting images to SVG

Another problem is one of converting images to an SVG. SVG means Scalable Vector Graphics, and in Cricut, it is a file that is designed mathematically, and it is entirely compatible with Cricut. When you use an SVG file for your images, you will have no problem with the appearance of your pictures.

It's not always easy to find images that are already in SVG format, and so you will have to convert it to SVG using an online tool.

Luckily, many online tools convert PNG and JPG files to SVG, although not all of them work perfectly.

Uploading images on Cricut

There is another problem of how to upload your designs and pictures. This is only possible with a Cricut Access Subscription. With this, you can use images that are not provided for you in Cricut Design Space.

Rest assured because you can always upload your images on your user-friendly Cricut Design Space.

Firstly, make sure that the picture you want to use does not need you to take permission before using it. It's safer to use pictures that you have rights to. When searching Google for images, you have to check out for the photos that you can use without asking for permission.

Also, the files have to be either .jpg, .png, .bmp, or .gif. These images can be edited while the uploading process is going on. If you don't find them, you can use .svg and .dxf files, although they are vectors. This means that as you upload, the layers will be separate.

Next, you open your canvas area to the design you want to add the image to or a blank page. Then you select if you're uploading an image or pattern fill. After that, choose if the image is complex, moderately complex, or simple.

Next, edit the picture so that it can flow with your design. Then, you click on continue; you will then choose if between 'print and cut' or just 'cut.'

If you think you will need your image again, you can save it to the application and use it at any time.

Your Cricut Design Space has stopped working

Every application, including Cricut Design Space, is prone to cashing, freezing or other challenges. There are some reasons why these problems can happen.

Slow internet

This is the most common problem with Cricut Design Space refusing to work. Before you get angry at Cricut, you should check your internet connection.

For the Cricut Design Space to work efficiently, it needs consistent internet speed. This means that both in the area of uploading and downloading, your internet speed must be up to par for your Cricut program to work ideally. If not, you will experience problems like freezing.

If your internet connection is slow, you should place your device close to your modem. If this doesn't work, you should contact your service provider.

The Browser

When using Cricut Design Space, your browser must be up to date to the latest version. You can use any browser when using Cricut. From Chrome and Mozilla to Firefox, any browser works as long as it's up to date.

If you're using a particular browser that is up to date and your Cricut Design Space isn't working, then you should switch to another browser. This usually works.

<u>Your device</u>

The problem can also be on the phone, tablet, or computer that you're using. For Cricut Design Space, there are some specified minimum requirements that your computer must meet.

<u>Apple Computers:</u>

Your Mac computer must meet the following requirements.

- A CPU of 1.83 GHz.

- Free 50MB space.

- Have 4GB RAM.

- Must be Bluetooth capable and have a USB port.

- It must be the Mac OS X 10.12 or something more recent.

<u>Windows Computers:</u>

Your Windows computer must meet the following requirements.

- It must feature an Intel Core series or AMD processor.

- Free 50MB space or more.

- Have 4GB RAM.

- Must be Bluetooth capable and have a USB port.

- It must be Windows 8 or a newer version.

If your system meets these requirements and your Cricut Design Space isn't working still, then it could be because of Background Programs.

You could clear your cache and history, update your system, check for malware, or update your antivirus.

Call Cricut Help Center

If all problems persist, then you call Cricut to fix the problem. The Design Space might be crashing or freezing because of an internal Cricut problem.

FAQ

Is there any software I can use that will allow me to use my own designs? Currently no third party software is compatible with Cricut. This wasn't always the case in the past and has made some unhappy Cricut users.

You can still manipulate designs by welding, kerning, flipping, rotating, grouping and shadowing your images. Visit YouTube and watch the helpful tutorials other crafters have posted to learn even more.

What types of material will a Cricut cut? Your Cricut will cut paper of various thicknesses. It will also cut card stock, vinyl, cardboard and cloth. But for each material you will need to adjust your settings. You may need to use the multi cut function for thicker material. Also, it's a good idea to switch to your deep cut blade for thicker material.

What is a Crop? This is just a get together for Cricut users and scrapbookers to share ideas and have fun.

I'm having trouble using the Craft Room with my Mac? Sadly, you're not alone. Provo Craft has supposedly worked out the issue regarding the security settings. It seems to happen most if Mac users have updated to Maverick on their Mac.

Can I have more than one computer authorized on my Craft Room account? Many people like to have their desktop and their laptop authorized for use in the Craft Room. This shouldn't be a problem since the Craft Room claims they allow two computers for each account. However, many users complain that they have to call customer service and unauthorize a computer every time they switch. This should not be the case; but apparently it is, at least for some users.

What types of projects can you create with a Cricut machine? The sky is the limit. Many people, like me, originally bought it for scrapbooking projects. We wanted to be able to cut out a multitude of shapes and designs.

Why can't I weed my design without it tearing? There are two fairly common causes for this type of issue. Number one is dull blades. The second reason is a build up of residues on your blades.

Is it necessary to turn all my images into SVGs? No, it is not necessary to convert your images to the SVG format if you have a JPG or PNG. However, if it is your wish to have SVG files in your project, there are several free online resources that can help you with this process. Try to keep in mind that if you convert your file type to an SVG, you may have less freedom to manipulate the components of your image.

Where do I go to buy materials? When it comes to buying materials for your Cricut, there are nearly an unlimited number of places where you can get them. Since the Cricut is such a versatile machine with the ability to cut so many materials, you won't be able to go into any crafting or fabric stores without tripping over new materials you can use for your latest and greatest crafts.

As you continue to learn more about how Cricut works and what you can do with it, you will find which materials and brands best suit your needs. From there, you will often find what you need by shopping online to get the best prices and quantities of the materials you prefer, which will help you stretch your dollar as best as you can.

Do I need a printer to use my Cricut? In a word, no. Using your Cricut doesn't require ink from a printer, though there are some materials on the market for Cricut, which are specifically meant to be printed on before using.

If you're not using these items, then you will find that you can get the most out of your machine without that feature.

If you wish to print things, then cut them, this is known as the Print then Cut method and there is a wealth of knowledge about this on the internet. You can make iron-on decals, tattoos, and so much more!

Where can I get images to use with my Cricut? The beautiful thing about the Cricut Design Space and its ability to host so many different file types, is that you can upload images from any source, so long as you have the legal rights to use that image. Pulling images off of Google Image Search is done amongst crafters, but if you're selling the design in any way, you will want to make sure that the images you're using are either open license, or you've purchased them for use and distribution.

Do I have to buy all my fonts through Cricut? Cricut Design Space has an option when looking through your fonts to use fonts that are installed on your computer. This is called "System Fonts." Ant font you can buy, or download can be used through Cricut Design Space with little to no issues. There are many resources for this on the internet as well.

However, if there is a font you're using, do make sure that you have the license to use the font for the purposes you have in mind for that font! Fonts, just like pictures, do have copyrights and can be limited in what they allow you to do with them.

Why is my blade cutting through my backing sheet? This can be due to improper seating on the blade in the housing, so just pop the housing out, re-seat the blade inside, reload, and try again. This can also be due to an improper setting on the material dial. If you're cutting something very thin, but have the dial set to cardstock, your needle could be plunging right through the whole piece of material and its backing!

Why aren't my images showing up right on my mat? It is possible, when you click "Make It," that the print preview of your project doesn't look anything like how you have it laid out in Design Space. If this is the case, go back to Design Space, highlight all your images, click "Group," then click "Attach." This should keep everything right where it needs to be for all your project cutting needs!

I'm just getting started, do I need to buy all of Cricut's accessories right away? No, you won't need all the accessories right at once, and some of them you won't ever need at all, depending on what crafts you intend to do with your Cricut machine. In fact, you can use crafting items you likely already have on hand to get started, buying tools and accessories here and there as you get more use out of your machine! It is, by no means, necessary to spend a small fortune on accessories and tools just to do your first Cricut crafting project!

Can I Use Design Space on My Chromebook? Unfortunately, Cricut's Design Space isn't currently optimized for compatibility with the Chromebook operating system. This is because the need to download the plugin for the application is a current barrier for that operating system, but this isn't to say there is no possibility for compatibility in the near future.

Can I use the Design Space on more than one of my devices? Yes, thanks to Cricut's web-based and cloud-based functionality, all of your designs, elements, fonts, purchases, and images are accessible from any device with an internet connection and your account credentials. This way, it's possible to start a design while you're out and about for the day, then wrap them up when you're back in your crafting space.

How many times can I use an image I buy in the Design Space? Any design asset or element you purchase through the design space is yours to use as many times as you'd like while you have an active account with Cricut Design Space! Feel free to cut as many of every image you'd like!

I accidentally welded two images. How do I unweld them? Unfortunately, there is no dedicated unweld option currently available in Design Space. If you weld an image, however, you can still click "Undo" if you have not saved the changes to your project. It is recommended that you save your images locally at each different stage, so you have clean images to work with for every project.

How do I set design space to operate on the metric system? On your computer (whether it's Windows or Mac), click the three stacked lines in the upper left-hand corner. From there, click "Settings." In those settings, you'll see the option to set inches or centimeters as the default measurement.

If you're using Design Space on your mobile device, you will access your settings from the bottom of your screen. You may need to scroll or swipe to the left to view all your options, but this setting is available on mobile as well!

What types of images can I upload through Cricut's design space iOS or Android apps? Any images that are saved in the Photos or Gallery app on your Apple or Android device can be uploaded! If you have SVG files saved, you can upload those as well.

If you are trying to upload a .PDF or a .TIFF file, it should be noted that Cricut Design Space does not support these.

Can I upload images through the Android app? Yes! Cricut understands how crucial mobile accessibility is to its users, so this feature has been made available on all platforms where you can access Cricut Design Space, including Android!

Select Upload in the bottom list of options, you may need to swipe to find it. Once you've tapped on that, select Open Uploaded Images. Once you're in your uploaded images, find the one you wish to delete. Tap the Info button, which is indicated with a green circle and a lowercase I. From here, you will be able to delete your image with ease!

Are the "despeckle" and "smooth" tools available in Design Space for Windows, Mac and Android? At the time of writing, these features are exclusive to the iOS platform. This means that only Apple devices have this feature, and there is currently no indication as to whether or not this is intended to change in the future.

What is SnapMat? SnapMat is an iOS-exclusive feature that allows you to give yourself a virtual mat preview. This gives you the ability to line up your designs in Design Space, so they'll fit perfectly onto what you have laid on your mat. This feature allows you to place images and text over the snapshot of your mat so you can see exactly how your layout should be in the Design Space.

What Are the Advantages to Using SnapMat? SnapMat gives you certainty in where your images will be placed when you send your design to cut through your Cricut. It will show you where your images will be drawn, cuts will be made, and how text lines up. With SnapMat, you can tell your Cricut to cut out a specific piece of a pattern you have stuck on your mat, write in specific areas of stationery, gift tags, envelopes, or cards, and you can get the absolute most out of your scraps and spare materials that are left from past projects!

Can I include multiple mats at one time with SnapMat? SnapMat can only snap one mat at a time. If you'd like to snap multiple mats, you can do so individually, and work through your designs that way. This ensures that each mat is shot properly and that each one is done with precision.

Can I save the snaps of my mat from the SnapMat feature? SnapMat doesn't currently have a "Save" feature for the images captured in it, so if you would like to retain a photo of your mat, simply take a screenshot in the middle of that process. This will save an image of your mat directly to your photo gallery.

If you find yourself referring to the image for where you have items on your may, it may be advisable to wait until you're ready to cut in order to take your snapshot.

How exact is SnapMat when it comes to where my cut lines will be? The SnapMat technology is quite precise and the lines should be accurate to within a tiny fraction of an inch. If possible, it's best to give yourself as much room as you can to allow for small deviations, but you can trust that the lines are overall very close to where they ought to be.

How can I be sure that SnapMat will work with the Cricut mat I have? SnapMat is compatible with all versions of the Cricut mats that are currently for sale. However, if you have a mat that is a bit older, or which has black gridlines, the app may have a little bit of a harder time differentiating between the grid and your design. It's best to do a couple of test runs with the mat you have, if it's not a Cricut brand mat, to ensure that everything will run smoothly.

What does it mean if SnapMat can't capture my mat? The capture feature of the SnapMat application will automatically capture the picture of your mat, once it's within view and it can detect it. If your app isn't detecting the mat, there could be a few things you need to check. The positioning of the mat is key, so make sure that's done properly, your hand is completely steady, and make sure that there is nothing else in the shot. If you're still having trouble, try these tips:

Add Contrast to Your Mat

If SnapMat can't easily see the difference between the edges of your mat and the surface behind it, you might have difficulty getting the picture to snap. Try laying a darker piece of fabric or material behind the mat so it has a lot of contrast to work with and see if that solves it!

Let There be Light!

If the lighting in your space is too soft or if there isn't enough of it, your camera could be having trouble picking up on the mat that's in front of it. Try adding more light to your crafting space, ideally the light should be placed behind the camera, aimed at the mat. When you're working with intricate projects such as these, having good lighting is best for your eyes, anyway!

Flatten the Mat

If your mat has any curling, or if your mat is unable to lie flat for any reason, the curvature or different in depth could alter the camera's perception of where items are on your mat. If you need to flatten your mat, consider placing it between to very heavy objects to flatten it.

Mind the Edges of Your Grid

The edges of your grid are part of what tell the SnapMat application where the materials are on your mat. So if you have materials that are hanging over the sides of your grid, you might find that your app is having trouble picking up where items are on your mat, or how large your mat actually is.

Look for the Green Square

Once SnapMat detects the edges around your mat, you'll see the green square or rectangle that indicates it's snapping the picture. If you're not seeing that rectangle, the picture has not been captured and further troubleshooting may be needed.

Keep it Level

The blue circles in the SnapMat application are a level. If you use those, ensure that the circles are even and this will tell you if your phone is level and thus, picking up a completely level and true photo of the mat in front of it. This will help you to be sure all the materials on your mat are captured in the right proportions.

My hands shake; how can I use SnapMat?

Don't worry, keeping the camera steady can be a real pain for a lot of users, so we've figured out a way around that. Many crafters have solved this by placing their mat on the floor, just under the edge of their table, while resting the phone or device on the tabletop, with the camera hanging over the edge. In most cases, this keeps your phone so steady that the snap is completed in mere seconds.

What is offline mode for Cricut Design Space? This is a feature that is exclusively available through the iOS platform. With this feature, you can download your items for use in an offline environment later. This is ideal if you're planning on working on your designs in a space that does not have an active internet connection for an extended period of time. In that time, you can still work on your designs without worrying about losing those creative thoughts!

Conclusions

If you have to add up all the time spent on perfecting lettering and cutting out intricate designs, patterns and slicing fondant with those pesky blades by hand. While there's nothing that beats homemade products, cards or personalized coasters, you can still personalize the same things with any of the Cricut machines and have the change to give them a professional and clean finish.

I have made hundreds of projects with my Cricut, and I am still learning every single day. It is like a computer; you will never learn every little trick in one goes. You will have to practice, follow the guide I have given, and add or scratch ideas out until you have your own. I hope that this handbook gave you at least a little head start, which I did not have back when I first started with the Cricut machines. Tomorrow I might learn something new, and I will kick myself for not adding that to this guide. Nevertheless, know that I have taught you every trick I know and shared every failure I have encountered in hopes that you can avoid it all and just start crafting like we all so desperately have wanted to do when we first got our Cricuts.

Never stop doing research. Never stop trying new things. Never, ever stop being creative. The Cricut does not make you any less creative; it just makes the process easier and efforts on more important things or personalizing the projects after making the cuts. It takes the tedious work out of your hands and makes everything fun, easy, and fast.

CRICUT DESIGN SPACE

Discover the principles behind cricut and learn how to craft beautiful designs for your home even if you are just a beginner. A step-by-step method with pictures and illustrations.

Introduction

A Cricut machine is considered a die-cutting machine. Today, they no longer have cartridges because they do not need them anymore. Now, everything is done digitally. This lets you use any font or shape that you want as long as it is on your computer. These machines are advanced now so they work over Bluetooth or Wi-Fi which makes it so that you can design straight from your iPad, your iPhone, or your computer, whichever is your personal preference.

The amazing thing is that, with a Cricut, you are only limited by your own creativity because there is so much out there for you to use. The Cricut is compared to a printer in some ways. When you have a printer, there is a design that you created on your computer and then you print it out. The difference is that, with a Cricut machine, you will cut the design out of whatever material you choose.

If you want to use the Cricut like a printer in whatever ways, you can do that as well. There is an accessory slot in your machine and you can load a marker into it. From there, you can load a marker into it and have the machine draw your design for you. It is great for getting a beautifully handwritten look. This is especially helpful to people whose handwriting is not considered a strong suit for them.

Each machine has different ways of cutting things, and you will notice this depending on which machine you get. You can make different things with them as well. You can cut fun shapes for scrapbooking (this is considered a lost art or an older generation activity but it is very entertaining and a great way for preserving memories) and design T-shirts, leather bracelets, stickers for your car, or envelopes. The options are endless, and all of them are fun and can be used as business options for people as well when you are creating your own designs.

This machine is great for precision cutting for crafting, but it is important to know that, while the paper is one of the many things that it can cut, it is not the only thing. They can also score material which makes folding easy and crisp to give it a professional look and it can write and draw with pens.

The Cricut machine also comes with its own app which makes it easier to make your own designs as well as uploading images. With the app, you can import cuts and purchase designs as well. It is easy to use and as such people find that it is a great way to be able to use your machine to its fullest extent.

These machines have been around for a few years now, and everything used to be done on cartridges. If you have an old Cricut cartridge, you should be able to use it for your new machine and your files should be intact and available for use. Now that it is done digitally, if you do not have a cartridge, you can have access to an enormous library of files for cuts. Along with the multitude of things it does, it can engrave as well. Engraving is a hot crafting want right now, and as such, many are jumping on the chance to learn it and utilize it for their benefit.

However, there are some warnings when you buy a Cricut machine. Most people highly recommend that you buy it directly from the website itself and not from a third party, particularly some of the more common retailers online. Now, most craft stores like Hobby Lobby or Joann are safe retailers, and you will get exactly what you are purchasing. However, there are downfalls to buying from the stores as well. The prices are generally higher than what you will find on the machine's own website, and you can't use coupons on any of the Cricut products. In addition to this, you will not find a bundle deal that could save you a lot of money and give you additional tools that you need.

Cricut has taken people by storm, and there are many benefits to buying one of these machines. The Explore and the Maker are both incredibly versatile that a lot of projects people use for blogs or social media come straight from one of these machines. People constantly use it for projects that never see the light of day, but many also use them for projects that they use in their everyday life and there are plenty more ideas that you can use that make you want to craft daily which shows what a great opportunity this machine can bring you. As many people will know and are aware of, while crafters do make a lot of projects that never see the light of day, they make just as many that do, and with the save option that this machine offers you, you can always go back to those projects later and improve on them before finishing them. This can be a great option for you if a holiday has come up and you do not have a gift, or if there are last-minute events that are coming up and you need cool ideas to take to them as well. Many of the projects on this machine are very quick and very small so they do not take up much time and do not take up many materials, which is a great option if you are a busy person and you do not have that much time to craft but you still want something amazing to do.

In addition to this, another benefit of buying a Cricut machine is that it will save you so much time. This is particularly true if you are used to hand-cutting. This machine can do it so much faster and will save your hands from cramping and you from dealing with frustration. You get to do projects that you have never even thought about doing because there is no way that you can do the intricate cuts by hand. The ability to make your custom projects is a great benefit as well because you can upload your designs and your pictures. Everything that you make can be personalized to exactly how you want it to be and exactly how you need it. You can also personalize gifts, and one of the best benefits that people have said is that it is easy to learn. People can be a little overwhelmed with the machines because they come with so much, but it is super easy for people to use Design Space because it is user-friendly and there's a lot of make it now projects that have a very easy learning curve.

There are more advanced things that you can do with these machines, but there are tutorials all over the Internet as well as books just like this one that can help you understand how to navigate the machine and how to navigate more advanced projects.

The Cricut does projects with a better accuracy and they look more professional. It also saves you headaches because you will not be wasting as much material, and it is a lot faster than crafting by hand so you gain time. Many people that have been crafting their whole life by hand understand said that this is a great machine because you are not only saving time but you are also saving yourself from unneeded pain that can cause permanent problems later on in your life that you do not need or want to happen.

There are a few cases where you might want to hold off on buying a Cricut because if you do not have a desire to be a maker, and you feel that you can just buy things off of a website because you do not feel like making it yourself, then you are not going to use your machine. This is not true for everyone, but it can be applied to some. You have to have some desire to want to make things yourself to use this machine. If you do not feel like making anything yourself, then you will not be using this machine to its potential; it will just be sitting unused.

If you just want to buy things because they look cool, this is going to be tricky for you as well. Many people buy things because they look cool, but then, they never use them so you will be buying a machine and the products and tools that go with it, but if you just buy it because it looks cool then you might not be using it. For something that looks cool, this machine can get expensive with everything that goes with it. In a case like this, instead of splurging on something that you will not use, splurge on something that you will. However, if you think this looks cool and you have a strong desire to make things yourself, this would be a perfect thing for you to get for yourself. What we are saying here is, to be honest with yourself. If you love the idea of this machine but you know you are never going to take it out of the box and use it, then this probably is not for you. But, if you know that you think this machine is one of the coolest things you have ever seen, and you can't wait to use it or see what it can do, this would probably be a really good purchase.

If you love cutting things by hand, this is also another reason that you should avoid getting a machine like this because, with a Cricut machine, very little will be cut by you.

What sets the Cricut machine apart from other machines in the same category is that they have several benefits that the others do not. These machines are perfect for people that do a lot of sewing and love making patterns or just love looking just at them. These machines are great because they make crafting more accessible for everyone even if you cannot craft daily. An example would be if you have been sidelined because of an injury or an illness. This machine can take over some of the more difficult tasks and they can bring you back to a hobby that you love and that you enjoy.

They have an adaptive system that allows it to cut with more power than other machines which means that you will be getting more use out of this machine and you can cut with entirely new materials that you have not been able to cut with before. You also do not have to have a huge pile of work in progress projects that are sitting on a shelf and never be finished if you choose the quicker ones that they offer. The Maker, in particular, has so much to offer and it has ready-to-make projects which means that you could make a project in literally under ten minutes if you wanted to. As handmade creations are coming back and more people are wanting to see them come back, this is the perfect way to take your crafting into the next movement to bring back art that many people have thought was lost.

One of the things that many people are not aware of about these machines is that if you cancel your subscription and you have images that you had saved for later use or have purchased when you cancel the subscription, you no longer have access to those images. So if you need them before you cancel your subscription, you should note that this is something to consider because if you ever decide not to keep the subscription, then you are losing a lot of projects that you have either wanted to complete or going to complete because you will not have the necessary image to do so. Another problem that people have with a Cricut machine is that they glitch, and when they glitch, it is mostly an Internet problem, but some of the glitches have been a little bit odder than other ones. When you get a glitch, that is not normal and lesser known. You will either have to spend time looking around on the Internet for a solution or you will have to call the company itself. However, if you have to call the Cricut company, you have the benefit of having a 50% less waiting time than the other customers, so calling the company itself is not considered a bad thing. The Cricut machine is an amazing machine and a great way to have fun with your crafts.

What Is Cricut Design Space?

Cricut Design Space is the online stage that Cricut designed to be utilized with their more up to date machines.

It's not programming – you download a module on your PC (or the application on your table/telephone), and after that, you can design however much you might want.

You can utilize designs and pictures that are now transferred into Design Space, or you can transfer your own!

Cricut Design Space is 100% free. You do need to make a record; however, if you would prefer not to, you don't need to spend a penny.

Cricut Design Space is an online programming program that enables you to interface with your cutting machines by means of USB or bluetooth. It's the way you make the majority of the wonderful designs that will wind up on your tasks, shirts, cushions, espresso cups, and the sky is the limit from there!

As an option in contrast to making your own designs or getting them from Cricut, I regularly shop at Etsy (simply scan what you're searching for with SVG toward the end) and afterward "play with" my designs. You can perceive how I do this in the video underneath, which additionally incorporates a fast stroll through presentation of Design Space:

While they have some free pictures and textual styles incorporated with the program, there are ones that you can pay cash for. You can likewise pursue a Cricut Access Plan, which will give you access to a great many pictures and textual styles.

Be that as it may, you can introduce your own textual styles onto your PC and transfer pictures to Design Space (that you've made, found for nothing, or obtained without anyone else).

Cricut Design Space is an online program, so you don't download it onto your PC.

Nonetheless, you should download some modules, which should auto popup and brief you to download when you experience the underlying procedure.

If you are needing to download Cricut Design Space onto your iPhone or iPad, then you will simply need to go to the Apple App Store, scan for "Design Space," and it ought to be the primary alternative to spring up. Download it like you regularly would.

Any undertaking that you make in Design Space can be spared to the Cloud. You simply need to ensure you spare your venture – that catch is in the upper right hand corner.

This enables you to see your task on any gadget where you are signed in.

Nonetheless, if you are dealing with an iPhone or an iPad, you have the choice to spare it just to your gadget. I would, for the most part, consistently propose sparing it to the Cloud, however!

You can utilize Design Space on Mac PCs, PC PCs, and iOS gadgets.

Your PC must run a Windows or Mac working framework, and hence, Google Chromebooks CANNOT be utilized, as they keep running on a Google OS.

Once in a while when you go to cut your design, it will stop you before you at the tangle see page and state you have to pay.

You may have incidentally included a picture that requires installment – you can return to your canvas and check each picture to check whether there is a dollar sign beside it (or check whether the text style you chose has a dollar sign. Remember that regardless of whether you have Cricut Access, you don't approach ALL the pictures and textual styles).

If you chose a venture from Design Space, it might have incorporated a picture or textual style that is paid. When you take a gander at the task guidelines, it should let you know if it is free or not.

I see this inquiry all the time in Design Space, and it very well may be so disappointing! Frequently, Design Space is down when they are making refreshes.

Some of the time, they will convey an email when they anticipate a blackout. However, I don't generally observe this.

If it's down, I would propose not reaching their client backing and simply be quiet. You can likewise attempt another program or clear your program store, just to ensure it is anything but an issue on your end.

Cutting is one of my preferred highlights in Cricut Design Space! I cherish removing text styles and pictures in different designs.

Yet, now and then it won't work. If you are observing this to be an issue, here are a couple of thoughts:

– Make sure the picture/text style you are removing of (so that is over another picture) is totally inside the other picture. If a bit of it is standing out, it won't cut.

– Make sure everything is chosen.

– Keep as a main priority that when you cut it, you will have two layers to expel from the picture – the first picture/text style that you cut, just as the cut

For what reason isn't Print and Cut working?

I won't jump a lot into Print and Cut, as it is a monster all alone.

Notwithstanding, the most compelling motivation why I see individuals experiencing difficulty with Print and Cut is that they didn't smooth their pictures! Before you go to print and cut, ensure you select all and press straighten.

For what reason Can't I Open Cricut Design Space?

Regularly you will get a blunder or a white screen with Design Space if you don't have the most as of late refreshed module.

If you get a clear page, take a stab at invigorating the page to check whether the module update shows up. Try not to move far from this page when it's refreshing, or it will turn white.

Cartridge

Designs are produced using parts put away on cartridges. Every cartridge accompanies a console overlay and guidance booklet. The plastic console overlay demonstrates key determinations for that cartridge as it were. Anyway as of late Provo Craft has discharged an "All inclusive Overlay" that is perfect with all cartridges discharged after August 1, 2013. The motivation behind the all-inclusive overlay is to simplify the way toward slicing by just learning one console overlay as opposed to learning the overlay for every individual cartridge. Designs can be removed on a PC with the Cricut Design Studio programming, on a USB associated Gypsy machine, or can be legitimately inputted on the Cricut machine utilizing the console overlay. There are two kinds of cartridges shape and textual style. Every cartridge has an assortment of imaginative highlights which can take into consideration several different cuts from only one cartridge. There are as of now more than 275 cartridges that are accessible (independently from the machine), containing textual styles and shapes, with new ones included monthly. The Cricut line has a scope of costs, yet the cartridges are compatible, despite the fact that not all alternatives on a cartridge might be accessible with the littler machines. All cartridges work just with Cricut programming, must be enrolled to a solitary client for use and can't be sold or given away. A cartridge obtained for a suspended machine is probably going to wind up futile at the point the machine is ended. Cricut maintains whatever authority is needed to suspend support for certain renditions of their product whenever, which can make a few cartridges quickly out of date.

The Cricut Craft Room programming empowers clients to join pictures from different cartridges, consolidate pictures, and stretch/turn pictures; it doesn't take into account the formation of discretionary designs. It additionally empowers the client to see the pictures showed on-screen before starting the cutting procedure, so the final product can be seen in advance.

Refering to Adobe's surrender of Flash, Cricut declared it would close Cricut Craft Room on 15 July 2018. Clients of "heritage" machines were offered a markdown to refresh to models good with Cricut Design Space. Starting at 16 July 2018, Design Space is the main programming accessible to make projects. Design Space isn't perfect with cartridges once in the past bought for the Cricut Mini, which was power nightfall in October 2018.

Third-party

Provo Craft has been effectively unfriendly to the utilization of outsider programming programs that could empower Cricut proprietors to remove designs and to utilize the machine without relying upon its exclusive cartridges. In a similar audit of bite the dust cutting machines, survey site TopTenReviews identified being "restricted to cutting designs from a gathering of cartridges" as a noteworthy downside of the Cricut run;

however, the audit noticed that it could be an inclination for some.

Two projects which could once in the past be utilized to make and after that get Cricut machines to remove subjective designs (utilizing, for instance, self-assertive TrueType text styles or SVG group illustrations) were Make-the-Cut (MTC) and Craft Edge's Sure Cuts A Lot (SCAL). In April 2010 Provo Craft opened lawful activity against the distributers of Make-the-Cut, and in January 2011 it sued Craft Edge to stop the conveyance of the SCAL program. In the two cases, the distributers settled with Provo Craft and expelled support for Cricut from their items. The projects keep on being usable with other home cutters.

As indicated by the content of its lawful grumbling against Craft Edge, "Provo Craft utilizes different strategies to encode and cloud the USB correspondences between Cricut DesignStudio [a design program provided with the hardware] and the Cricut e-shaper, so as to secure Provo Craft's restrictive programming and firmware, and to avoid endeavors to capture the cutting commands". Provo Craft battled that so as to comprehend and imitate this darkened convention, Craft Edge had dismantled the DesignStudio program, in opposition to the provisions of its End User License Agreement, along these lines (the organization affirmed) breaking copyright law. Provo Craft additionally affirmed that Craft Edge were damaging its trademark in "Cricut" by saying that its product could work with Cricut machines. Provo Craft declared this was likely "to cause perplexity, misstep or double dealing with regards to the source or starting point of Defendant's merchandise or benefits, and [was] prone to erroneously recommend a sponsorship, association, permit, or relationship of Defendant's products and ventures with Provo Craft."

The consequence of this is clients with more seasoned variants of Cricut machines that were 'power dusk' by stopping of programming bolster have no elective programming to use with their now outdated machines.

Getting To Know Design Space

Cricut Beginners usually get discouraged when they open Cricut Design Space.

This is because there are a lot of icons and options that you need to learn. If you don't, you can even spoil a project with the wrong decision.

But once you understand what all the panels and icons are meant for, it will be easy to jump into a new project with confidence.

Cricut Design Space Canvas Area

Before you cut up your projects, the Canvas area is where all the designing and arts happen. Here, you can organize your project, upload images or fonts.

The Cricut Design Space is just similar to the other design programs that most of us are useful, like Adobe Creative Cloud, Photoshop, or Illustrator. And so, if you have any experience with these programs, then it won't be difficult for you to understand the Design Space.

So, the Canvas Area is where you edit and touch up your designs before cutting them, but because there are many options that might overwhelm you, we will be taking these options one-by-one to explain their uses.

The Canvas Area is made up of the Right Panel, Left Panel, Top Panel, and Canvas Area.

1. Right Panel

The Right Panel deals with layers, and so it can also be called the Layers Panel. Layers signify the designs that are on the canvas area. The number of layers that you use depends on the complexity of your design or the project that you're working on.

When making a birthday card, you will have texts and different decorations, and probably a picture or two. All of these are the layers of the design.

This panel allows you to create and manage layers when making a design. Every item that is on the layers panel will display the Fill or Line type that you are using.

• Group, Ungroup, Duplicate, and Delete.

These settings allow you to move different designs around the canvas area.

- Group: This allows you to group layers. When you have different layers that come together to make a complicated

167

design, you use this option to bring them together. For example, if you're making a house, there will be different parts of that house. A standard home will have a roof, door, walls, and windows. 'Group' allows you to arrange all the layers and ensure that they stay together when you're making a design.

- Ungroup: You can also separate a design of different layers, by clicking on this button. This is pretty much the opposite of 'Group'.

- Duplicate: As the name implies, this option will duplicate the layers that you select on the canvas.

- Delete: This option will delete any layer that you select and remove it from the canvas.

• Blank Canvas

This is also a layer in the Right panel that gives you the option of changing the color of the canvas. If you're experimenting with your design, you can use this option to place it against various backgrounds.

• Layer Visibility

This is represented by a little eye that is on every layer on the panel. It signifies the visibility of that layer or design. During designing, if you see that a particular segment or element doesn't look right, you can click on the eye to hide it. That way, you don't end up deleting it permanently if you decide to put it back. The hidden item can be identified with a cross mark.

• Slice, Weld, Attach, Flatten and Contour

It's important to learn how to use these five tools. No matter what you're designing, they will come in handy.

- Slice: This tool is meant for cutting out texts, shapes, and other elements from a whole design.

- Weld: This is used for combining shapes to make a new shape. If you want to do something different with your designs, you can join two or more shapes together.

- Attach: This is like a more powerful version of the Group option. It connects shapes and changes the color to match whatever background color that you're using. This will remain even after cutting.

- Flatten: This tool is useful when you're about to print two or more shapes. To do this, you should pick the layers that you want to print and select the Flatten option.

- Contour- If you want to hide a layer of design, or just a small part, you can use this option to do so. Although, you can only do this when your design has layers that can be taken apart.

- Color Sync

This option is meant for evening out the colors of your design and even background. You can use this to change different shades of a color to just one color. It synchronizes the colors, as the name implies.

2. Left Panel

The left panel includes all the options you need for inserting. You can add shapes, texts, images, even ready-to-cut projects.

With this panel, you can add everything that you plan on cutting. The panel has seven options, and we will explore them all.

- New

You select this option when you want to create a new page apart from the one that you're using to design.

It's advisable to save your designs before you move to the new page just in case you need it on another time. If not, you can lose your designs.

- Templates

A template is used to give you a feel of what your design will look like when you cut it out on a particular type of fabric like a t-shirt or a bag. If you're making an iron-on design on a bag, it will show you a picture of the bag, and you can place the design on the template so you can plan how it will look in real life.

Templates are great because they give you an idea of what your design looks like when cut out. It won't cut out an actual backpack for you.

• Projects

If you're ready to cut, then you should go to projects. You will pick your project, edit it, and tailor it to your tastes and click on the 'Make It' option.

A large number of the project available are available to Cricut Access members, or some are available for purchase. Apart from these, a few are free.

• Images

Images allow you to add a personal touch to your designs. With this option, you can insert pictures provided for you on Cricut Design Space.

Cricut even provides free images every week, although some come with Cricut Access.

• Text

The text option allows you to add a text to your design or just on the canvas area. It opens a small window telling you to add text, and so you can do that and customize the font and color.

• Shapes

You use this option when you want to add shapes to your canvas area. Cricut Design Space offers some shapes, namely triangle, square, pentagon, hexagon, octagon, star, and heart.

There is also the Score Line tool under the Shapes option. You can use this option to fold the shapes into different shapes, especially when you're making cards.

• Upload

The last tool in the Left panel is the Upload tool, which allows you to upload your files and images apart from those Cricut provides for you.

With this, you can upload images or patterns.

3. Top Panel

The top panel is the busiest panel. It has two different subpanels, and generally, the top panel is used for the general editing and organizing of elements and layers of design.

• First Subpanel

This allows you to name your project, save it, and eventually cut it. Here, you can navigate to saving, naming, and sending your project to the Cricut machine for cutting.

- Toggle Menu: This part of the subpanel allows you to manage your account and your account subscriptions. This menu also gives you the option of updating your Cricut Design Space, calibrating your machine and others.

- Project Name: You can use this to name your project. Your project will be automatically called 'Untitled' until you give it a name that you can use to identify it.

- My Projects: This is a library of all your projects saved on the Cricut Design Space, and so you can always refer to old projects.

- Save: This option saves your project into the library. As you work, you should save in case your browser crashes.

- Cricut Maker / Cricut Explore: When you're using Cricut Design Space for the first time, it asks you if you're using a Cricut Explore machine from the series or a Cricut Maker. Seeing as the Cricut Maker is a more advances machine, it provides more benefits on Design Space than the machines in the Explore series.

- Make It: After uploading your files, you click on Make It so that it can cut. The software will categorize your projects depending on their colors. Also, if you're planning to cut more than one project, you can use this to increase the projects that you want to cut.

• Second Subpanel

This subpanel is the editing menu. It allows you to edit, organize, and arrange images and fonts on the Canvas Area.

- Undo & Redo: You can click undo when you make a mistake or create something that you don't want. And, you can click on redo if you mistakenly delete something that you need.

- Cut under (Line type): All your layers on the canvas area have this line type. After selecting the Make It option, the Cricut machine cuts the designs on your canvas area. Cut under allows you to change the colors of the layers and the fill too.

- Draw (Line type): Cricut also allows you to write and draw on your designs. When you select this line type, you're given different options of different Cricut pens, and so, you can use these to draw on the canvas area.

Here, when you click on Make It, your Cricut machine will draw or write instead of cutting.

- Score (Line type): This is an advanced version of the Scoring Line in the left panel. When you select this option for a layer, the layer will look scored. And so, when you click on Make It, the Cricut machine will score the materials instead of cutting it. When you want to score, you will require a scoring stylus or scoring wheel. The scoring wheel can only work with the Cricut Maker.

- Engrave, Wave, Deboss, and Perf (Line type): These four tools are brand new! They were released by Cricut recently and they can only be used by Cricut Maker users. Also, that user has to have the latest version of the Design Space application. These tools allow you to have significant effects on a lot of materials.

- Fill: This is mainly used for patterns and printing. You can only use this option when Cut is selected as a line type.

- Print: Any Cricut user really likes this option. This allows you first print out your design, and then cut them out. To use the print option, when the fill option is active, you first click on Make It. And then, you send the files to your printer at home before feeding it into the Cricut for cutting.

- Edit: This icon contains three options on the drop-down menu. There is the cut option that allows you to remove an element from the canvas, the copy option which copies the same component without removing it and the paste option, which inserts the element that was cut or copied.

- Select All: You can use this to highlight everything on your canvas area.

- Align: There are different options under this, and it is important that you master all of them. They are:

- Align Left: This option ensures that all the elements are aligned to the left. The detail at the end of the left side will determine how the other details move.

- Center Horizontally: This will align all the elements horizontally.

- Align Right: This will align the elements to the right. As with align left, the item at the end of the left side will determine how the other items move.

- Align Top: This will align the elements you select to the top of the canvas page.

- Center Vertically: This will align all the design elements vertically.

- Align Bottom: This does the opposite of the Align Top option by aligning the layers or elements to the bottom.

- Center: This aligns both the horizontally aligned and vertically aligned elements to the center.

- Distribute: This allows you to create the same spacing between elements or layers.

Distribute Horizontally

Distribute Vertically

- Flip: If you want to reflect your designs as though they are looking at a mirror, you can use this option. It provides two options.

Flip Horizontal

Flip Vertical

- Arrange: The arrange options allow you to move elements like images, texts, or designs to the front or back of others. It provides four options.

- Send to Back: This will displace the selected designs or elements and take them to the back.

- Move Backward: If you select an element and click on this, the elements moves back once. If you have three parts, you can move one to the middle of the other two.

- Move Forward: this is the opposite and it moves the element forward once.

- Send to Front: This will displace the selected element and take it to the front.

 - Size: This provides you with the options to adjust, increase or decrease the size of the elements or total design. Everything that you create has a scale, and you use this to modify the size. This is especially if you have a specific format that you're following.

 - Rotate: The Cricut Design Space allows you to rotate the element or layer to any angle that you choose.

 - Position: Seeing as the canvas area has grid lines, you can use these options to pick a particular position for the element on the X and Y axis.

 - Font: For your projects, Cricut provides you with different fonts if you're using Cricut Access. If not, you can use your system's font or use the Cricut fonts for a price.

- Font Size: This allows you to increase or decrease the size of your font.

 - Line Space: This is especially useful when you want to ensure that your texts on your design are evenly spaced or spaced according to your preference.

- Letter Space: This allows you to arrange the spaces between the letters.

- Style: This includes Regular, which is the default setting. Bold, which makes the font thick. Italic, which tilts the font sideways. Bold Italic which combines both the Bold and Italic function.

- Curve: You can also design your texts by using the curve setting. You can curve your text upwards or inwards. You can also curve your texts into a circle.

- Advanced: On the top editing panel, this is the last option.

- Ungroup to Letters: This allows you to disconnect each letter into single layers each.

- Ungroup to Lines: This allows you to disconnect a paragraph on different lines.

- Ungroup to Layers: This is a very tricky option, and it's only available on Cricut Access or if you purchase it.

4. Canvas Area

This is the main workspace of the Cricut Design Space. Here, you have all the elements and designs that you're working on.

- Canvas Grid and Dimensions

Grid lines cover your canvas area on the Cricut Design Space and separate the area into small squares. The canvas area looks like the cutting mat, so you will feel like you're designing on your cutting mat on the screen.

You can use inches or centimeters, and you can turn off the grid in your settings.

• Zoom Out or In

You can use this to zoom in or out on your canvas area. If you want to make a design bigger so you can work on it, or just an element, you can use this option.

• Selection

When you select a layer or more, the selection color is blue, and four corners around it allow you to modify the layer. There is an X that is colored red; you click on this when you want to delete the layers.

Mastering the Different Panels and Their Icons.

• The Editing Panel.

The editing panel is at the top of your Canvas Area. It harbors the controls that makes it easier for you to work around a project.

The editing panel is divided into two subpanels.

- <u>Subpanel One</u>: Allows you to create, name, save, and cut a project

- <u>Subpanel Two</u>: Gives you all the editing tools.

Setting Up Your Cricut Machine On Design Space

I am going to help you set up your machine and we will make it as easy as possible so that this will not only go smoothly but so that you can enjoy your machine without frustrating yourself. There are two different ways to do this and it depends on what technology you are working with. If you are working with a Mac or a Windows you need to set it up one way, and if you are running on an Android or an iOS you will have to do it another way. Many people think that this process is hard but it's actually quite simple and takes ten steps or less which is great right? How easy is that?

However, in case the door does not open automatically, put mild pressure on it to completely open the door. Then, place the keyboard overlay on the top of the keypad of the machine. At this point, the cartridge of the machine should be inserted into the cartridge slot.

The cartridge slot can be found in the front of the Cricut machine. However, you must ensure the title on the cartridge is in consonance with the one on the keypad overlay.

The first way we will show you how to how to set up your machine if your working with an Android or an iOS. This can be a very frustrating thing when you are trying to set things up and this is something that we want to avoid. So let's get started so you can get your machine ready.

Plug Your Machine In And Turn The Power On.

You will need to pair your device (either Android or iOS) with your machine. You are going to need to utilize your Bluetooth to do this.

Download the Design Space App. You will need to install it into your machine as well.

Hit the Button That Says Menu.

Select the button that says machine setup and app overview. Now, you are going to select the button that says new machine setup.

The next step is pretty simple because the only thing that you will have to do is follow what your screen says. There are going to be on-screen promptings that will help you to complete the setup. Just be sure that you are following them accurately and if you can't go quickly that's fine. Go at the pace that your comfortable with so that you can make sure that you understand what it is they are wanting from you. Going slower will help eliminate mistakes but if you do make mistakes don't feel bad. This happens to people every day and it's easily fixable.

You will know that you've done everything right and correctly when it is telling you that it's time to make your first project. Once this happens, you know that your setup is complete. Once you've done this it's time to get crafting!

An additional tip for you is that your machine is already automatically registered during the setup. If you don't complete the setup when you connect your machine you need to reconnect it. Because the machine has to be registered this is something that you can't miss.

If you're working with a Windows or a Mac you will need to follow these following instructions to make your machine work. This setup is easy as well and offers one less step than the instructions above and since Macs are considered to be newer this will be a little bit different than the instructions above.

Plugin your machine. Don't turn your machine on or try to without plugging it in first.

Power The Machine On

Connect your machine to your computer. You are going to do this in two different fashions. This is a great option because you can choose which option is the best for you. You can either do this by using the USB cord and do it this way or you can connect your machine by pairing it by using Bluetooth. Either of these ways will work well it's just whatever you would like it to be.

Go to the website design.cricut.com/setup in your browser because this is going to be how you are going to finish your set up. From this step, you will be able to complete your setup by making sure you are watching the instructions carefully.

You need to be able to follow the on-screen prompts and instructions to sign in and create your ID. This will be your Cricut ID for the future.

Download the Design Space app and install it to the device. This is going to have so much benefit for you later as this is where you are going to gain a lot of benefits.

Don't forget that you will need to plugin when it prompts you to do so.

You will be able to see that you did everything right and correctly when it wants you to make your first project. Once you reach this step your machine is ready to go, and you can make the practice project so that you can get used to your machine and how it works without wasting materials.

The same tip above about the registration applies here too and if you have a problem setting up on any of the systems you can come back to this site so that you can be able to set it up without trouble or issues. Having the website tell you what you need to do and having the prompts is a great helper to new users or older users of the machine as they offer help pages as well. With simple steps and back up help however starting your machine is easy as can be which is a great benefit to the user. These models are made to be as user-friendly as possible to eliminate the issues that other companies have when their items are being set up.

By now you should have the app installed on your phone or the software already running on your laptop or desktop computer. If you have not yet, you better do so now because things are about to get a lot more serious, and it would help if you have Cricut Design Space in front of you to experiment what we will be discussing.

What's more, you should do this, especially if you are a beginner. Perhaps intermediaries or fairly experienced users can afford not to have the app or software in front of them right now.

Downloading/Installing

Do you actually know where to get the Cricut Design Space? Well, if you are on a desktop or Personal Computer, navigate to https://design.cricut.com. If you are using an iOS device such as an iPhone or iPad, find your way to your App Store and input "Cricut Design Space" on the search space.

If your smartphone runs on Android OS, enter the Play Store and use the same search term. Remember that downloading or installing this is completely free of charge. Also, bear in mind that you will be needing a Cricut ID to sign in. This you can also get for free, even if you do not have a Cricut. Simply follow the prompts provided.

Once you have entered your email and gotten your ID, you will at once be taken into the main domain of the Cricut Design Space, the place where all of the magic happens. Quick tip: bookmark this page to your web toolbar so you can find it easily whenever you want to.

The Canvas you will be shown after - similar to a painter's whiteboard - is the big space where all your designs and progress will reflect - this space has a full grid by default to allow you see everything about a single work without having to pinch-zoom and un-pinch. Nevertheless, you can choose the appearance and measurements of the grid.

<u>Smart Guides And Shortcuts</u>

So you want to try out your first design, and you happen to be stuck while trying to perfectly position something on your canvas? In Cricut Design Space, this could happen because the Smart Guides are just too smart for their own good. Want to know what the guides are about?

Quick one: Smart Guides are a feature of the Android and iOS app version of the product. They are designed to help you when you want to position things in relation to other things. But that could not turn out or position the way you want it to. If you want to turn this off on the app version, go to Settings - at the bottom areas of the toolbar - and toggle the Smart Guides off.

Meanwhile, there's something about the desktop version of Cricut Design Space that makes it somewhat cool - it has some keyboard shortcuts that will definitely come in handy. If you want to see them at any point of use, tap on the question mark key on your keyboard - Shift + . Shortcuts that will prove useful to you include the showhide menu, toggle grid, and select all options.

Other shortcuts also allow you to save and "save project as", undo - this is something you will be thankful for - redo, cut, copy, and paste. What's more, bring forward, send back, bring to front, send to back, and of course, delete.

If you are the kind of technophile who's more used to the keyboard than clicking on a mouse, you will find these shortcuts super useful.

How To Position Items On The Cricut canvas

Not to discourage anyone, but it can take you several months of using the Cricut Design Space almost every day before you will find this useful, and probably a little more time before you can get used to it.

Well, this little nugget actually informs you on how to move and rotate your items on the mat preview. This is done in order to position your cuts and pen write when you want or feel the need to.

You know when you are working on a project and just want to flip things up fast? This feature lets you do so quickly and effortlessly - well, almost (insert smirk emoticon here).

This comes significantly handy when you want to use up scraps and just spread them all over your canvas. If you are working on an address envelope, for instance, you can use this tool so that your letters reflect on the "write" side on the envelope. You may also want to reposition - do so by tapping and dragging an item on your canvas to a new location. Simple enough, isn't it?

On the desktop version, move the objects to another mat and conceal them altogether - just click on the three dots, they are not hard to find since they are virtually in your face. So, now you know how to best position those items to make your design all the more easier. Now, on to the next on our list.

Do You Want To Sync Your Colors?

Even newbie designer knows the essence and impact of colors. In Cricut Design Space, you need to make sure your colors are happy and in harmony, just like every other artwork.

If you have ever worked on a design that had up to five different shades of pink that all needed to be cut out on separate pieces of paper or vinyl, you would understand what we are talking about. If not, you will understand soon too.

Well, in case you do not know or probably forgot how it feels, it can be very frustrating. It becomes ironic when you develop a red face that terribly matches with the moment.

Thanks to the syncing color feature, you can get all these shades and tint to match one another. Use the Color Sync option in the desktop version by simply clicking on "Color Sync" which appears at the top of the panel on the right side.

When you do this, Cricut Design Space will show you all the colors being used in your project, and then you will be able to manage them in the best possible way.

For Android and iOS users, tap on the Sync icon in the lower toolbar to have access to the same set of options. Color-syncing makes you work look more unified and professional, by the way.

Showing Others What You Are Working On

You would want others to have a sneak peek at your design in Cricut. If you have followed design freaks and enthusiasts, you would want to show them what you have been able to whip up, probably to tell you what you should add and remove.

Well, sharing is very possible, as long as the canvas on which you are currently working does not contain any uploaded files such as SVG files. Also make sure that you have not disabled the "Public" option.

If all these things are in place, then absolutely nothing is stopping you from sharing your design, except, of course, you change your mind.

First, make sure you have saved the project. Navigate the Cricut Design space to your Saved Projects location. Find the project you want and click on the Share option.

This will automatically provide you with a link you can send to people you want to see the project. It is just like the conventional infogram share option everyone is using nowadays. You can share your design with others only on the desktop and iOS version.

We are still waiting for the developers to include the same option in the Android app version of the design. But before that, sharing is easy as peasy, and I am sure Android's child will be too.

How To Remove Parts Of A Current Design

Many Cricut Design Space users have taken to social media to ask how they can remove some bits of their design when they do not want it. Actually, when you do not know what to do and how, this can be a hard nut to crack. But not for any longer.

You can remove some fragments of your progressing or finished design whenever you want, because the space has a feature that lets you do so. This feature is called Contour - you may have come across this somewhere and did not have the slightest idea that this is what it is used for. Or maybe you have not come across it at all.

192

To use it, just open your design in Cricut Design Space and click on the Contour button - you will see this description in the lower part of the right corner on your desktop. If you are using the mobile application version, tap on Actions, and you will see the Hide Contour option.

What next? Simply tap or click (on both app and desktop, respectively perhaps) on the bits you want to remove, and Cricut Design Space will do the rest by hiding them. Remember to save the changes once you are done "editing." This feature often works best on the desktop and iOS app versions. So if you are using the Android-based model, this should give you a heads up.

Uploading Personal Images And Rearranging Layers

Well, JPG, PNG, GIF, and BMP images can be used in the Cricut Design Space. What's more, you can easily remove the background if you want to.

This comes in very handy when you want to get nearly any kind of shape for the cutting you desire. What do you do? If you do not have the image already, look up for some of your choicest online.

When you find the one that works for you, go ahead to upload it on your canvas. There are clean up tools available for you to clean up the background to prevent interference with your project. This feature has no version bounds, as it works both on desktop and app versions (both iOS and Android).

When it comes to rearranging your layers, Cricut Design Space also has you covered. Case in point, you could just be working on a wedding invitation card projects, and you will find that the parts are overlapping.

This can cover up bits of the design you need to see to make sure you are getting it right. Well, this is something that can be fixed. Select the exact object and click Arrange, after which you should choose the Move Backward or Move Back option.

If you are using the desktop version, tap on Edit > arranged > Move Backward. Whatever be the mischief, it will surely be managed. You can now go on with your work without the layers poking out into your eyes.

If you invest in a Cricut and do not know how to master the Design Space, the investment will be futile. You will always need this software before you can think of actually cutting anything.

Tools In Cricut Design Space

Mastering the different panels and their icons.

<u>The editing panel.</u>

The editing panel is at the top of your Canvas Area. It harbors the controls that makes it easier for you to work around a project.

The editing panel is divided into two subpanels.

- Subpanel One

- Subpanel Two.

Subpanel one allows you to create, name, save, and cut a project.

Subpanel two gives you all the editing tools.

- <u>Subpanel one.</u>

The Subpanel one has few icons on it. Lets get the icons explained.

- Canvas: I refer to this as the main button on the design space area. A click on the icon/button and a drop down menu will appear with a range of options. From the drop down menu you can do a lot of settings.

Home
Canvas
New Machine Setup
Calibration
Manage Custom Materials
Update Firmware
Account Details
Link Cartridges
Cricut Access
Settings
Legal
New Features
United States ▾
Help
Sign Out

From this drop down menu you can manage your profile. Also, you can calibrate your machine, update firmware, link cartridges, etc. If you have a premium access to Cricut design space, you can manage your subscription from the drop down menu. I always advise beginners to take their time and click on all the options on the drop down menu to understand their functionalities.

- Project Name: In Cricut design space, all new project are by default 'Untitled.' You can only give a project a name when you have started working on it either by placing an element, or a text on it.

- My Projects: A click on this icon will lead you to all your prior designs if you have any.

- Save: This icon becomes functional when you have started working on a project. It is always advisable that you save your project as you design should in case of anything going wrong. I learnt this the hard way. During my early days with Cricut, I'd only save when I was done with a project until one day, I was about done with a particular project when my browser crashed and that was it with my project. I couldn't recover it because I never saved.

- <u>Maker (Machine)</u>: This icon has two sub-options when you click on it. The two sub-options include, Cricut Maker and Cricut Explore Family. Depending on the machine you are using, you will need to select either of the sub-options while working. These two options have different tools.

- <u>Make It</u>: When you are done designing and uploading your projects, this is the final icon you click on to have your project cut.

When you click on Make It, there will be a display on your screen which shows the different colors of your project. From the displayed window you can perform other functions like increasing the number of projects to cut, etc. When you are done with your selection, you can click on Continue to proceed.

- <u>Subpanel Two (Editing Menu)</u>

The image above represents the editing panel of the Cricut design space. I will take the icons one after another and explain their functions and usefulness. I lettered the different icons to make it easier for better understanding.

198

The Undo and Redo: This is a very important icon in your design canvas. This icon helps you make corrections either by taking you back or forward a bit.

Whenever you are designing, there is every possibility that you will make mistakes. With the undo and redo option, when you delete something by mistake, clicking redo will bring it back. When you make a mistake in your design space, clicking undo will get out.

Linetype and Fill: The linetype and Fill icon tells your machine the tools, and blades you are going to use for cutting your project. There are seven options on the Maker Linetype, these includes Cut, Draw, Score, Engrave, Deboss, Wave, and Perf. On the Cricut Explore Family linetype, there are just three options.

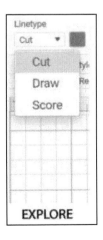

Explaining the Linetype options tools.

- Cut: This is the default linetype of all element on your canvas, except you upload a PNG or JPEG image. When you press Make It at the end of your design, this prompts your machine to CUT those designs.

The cut option also help you change the fill of elements in your project. These elements translates into colors of materials which you will use when cutting your project.

- Draw: This tool on the linetye helps you write on your design. When you select this option, you will be prompted to choose any of the Cricut pens available for you. Upon selection of a particular pen, the layers on your canvas area will be listed with the color of the pen you picked.

When the DRAW tool is selected and you click on MAKE IT, your Cricut will either write or draw instead of cutting. Also, this option doesn't color your designs at all.

- Score: The Score tool is an important version of the scoring line which is located on the left panel of your canvas space. When this tool is selected and assigned to a layer, all the designs will appear dashed or scored

At the end of your project when you click on MAKE IT, your Cricut will score the materials instead of cutting them.

- Engrave, Deboss, Wave, And Perf: These are new tools added by Cricut to the Cricut Maker Machine. With these tools you will be able to create amazing designs of different materials. They are still pretty new, so try them out when you can.

One thing I know for sure about these tools is that they work with the Quick Swap Adaptive Tool.

The FILL tool

This option/tool is used mainly for patterns and printing. The Fill option gets activated only when you are using CUT as a linetype. When you have 'No Fill' it means that you won't be printing any project.

The Print tool is about the most important tool on your design canvas because it makes it possible for you to print your projects and cut them.

When the Fill tool is active, when you click MAKE IT, firstly, the files will be sent to your printer while your Cricut do all the cutting.

The Print have two sub-options that allows you to perform magic on your canvas. These options includes the 'Color, and Pattern.'

When you explore these options you will be amazed at the project you will create.

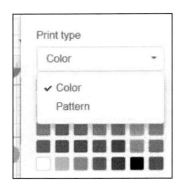 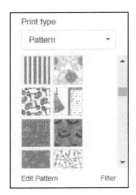

Select All: This tool serves to help you select all the element in your canvas area. Sometimes it is a hassle to select elements individually, so this tool helps you make multiple selections at a time.

Edit: The Edit icon when clicked on have three tools, the CUT, COPY, and PASTE. With these options, you can copy an element, paste a copied element, or cut off an unwanted element on your canvas.

Once you have made a selection on your canvas, the cut and copy tool gets activated. When you have copied or cut an element, the PASTE option gets activated.

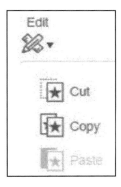

The Align Icon: If you have ever used another design tool, this will be an easy walk around for you. But if you have not, its easy to get a hang of.

The alignment icon is one you should master as it is very important while working on your project. The alignment tool helps your project stay perfectly organized and in line.

The Align icon has a drop down menu that contains other alignment tools.

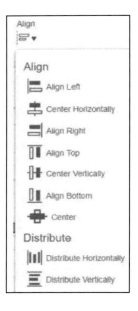

Lets take a look at what the functions on the align drop down means.

- Align: This particular tool allows you to align all the elements in your design. It is activated when you select two or more elements on your canvas.

- Align Left: This function takes all the selected elements and align them to the left. Whichever element that is furthest at the left determines the alignment.

- Center Horizontal: Just like every other alignment option, this will align all the elements on your project horizontally while the texts and images are centered.

- Alight Right: When you activate this option, all the elements on your project will be aligned to the right. Whichever element that is furthest at the right determines the alignment.

- Alight Top: this options aligns all the elements of your project to the top. Whichever element that is furthest at the top determines the alignment.

- Center Vertically: With this option, all the elements of your project will be aligned to the center. When working with columns and you want them organized and properly aligned, use this option.

- Align Bottom: This alignment option will align all the selected element on your project to the bottom. Whichever element that is furthest at the bottom determines the alignment.

- Center: When this option is clicked on, it perfectly centers every element on your project; shapes, text, images.

- Distribute: The distribute option gives equal spacing to all the element on your project. In Cricut design, there is nothing as time consuming as trying to manually allocate equal space between the elements on your project so with this tool, all your problems are solved. For this tool to be activated, two or more elements must be selected on your project.

- <u>Distribute Horizontally</u>: This option will distribute the elements on your project horizontally. The furthest elements left and right on your project will determine the length of the distribution.

- <u>Distribute Vertically</u>: This option will distribute the elements on your project vertically. The furthest elements left and right on your project will determine the length of the distribution.

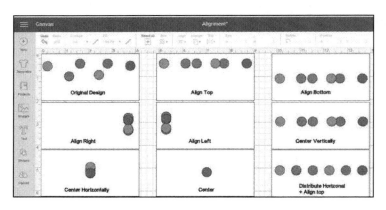

<u>Arrange</u>: The Arrange option helps put the elements on your project the right place. When you are working on a project with multiple text, images, and deigns, there is every probability that the new elements you add will be placed in front of others, but,

206

in actual sense you want them placed at the back. The arrange option makes it easier to do that.

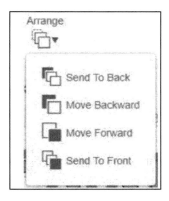

The Arrange option has other sub-options which includes:

-       Send Back: This action will move all selected element on your project to the back.

-       Move Backward: This action will move all selected elements on your project one step back. This simply means that activating this item will just take the element(s) only one step back instead of all the way back behind other elements.

-       Move Forward: This action will move selected element(s) a step forward.

-       Send to Front: This action will move selected element(s) to the front of every other element on the project.

FLIP: The Flip icon gives you the ability to reflect your designs on your Cricut canvas.

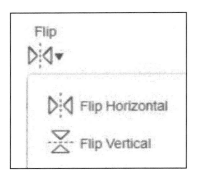

The Flip option has two sub-options:

-   Flip Horizontal: This action when activated reflects the images on your design horizontally . The best way I can explain this to you is that, Flip horizontally helps you duplicate a design. When you have a design at the right and want to duplicate same design at the left, Flip horizontally helps you with that.

-   Flip Vertical: This action perfectly helps you create a shadow effect on your design by flipping the selected design vertically.

Size: Every element you introduce to your design canvas (text, image, shape) has a size. Sometimes you may not want to alter the size, but, the Size icon gives you the ability to modify elements to any size of your choice.

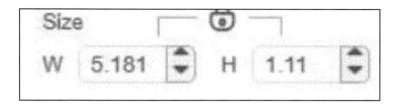

After modifying the size of an image, it is essential to click the lock icon on the size option. This is tell your Cricut program that you don't want to keep that same dimensions as default.

Rotate:

The rotate action helps you rotate an element to your desired angle. It can get tedious trying to get an image on your project to the right angle manually, but with the rotate option, it is very easy.

Position: This option shows you exactly where your elements are on a design canvas area. With this tool you can move elements on your project around by specifying where you want them to be.

This is pretty much an advanced tool, but a similar option to this is the alignment tool.

Font: This option gives you access to the different text fonts available for your design on Cricut. You can choose any font of your choice to work with.

<u>Style</u>: The Style option works in hand with Fonts. Once you select a font of your choice, the next step is to choose the style. The style option has some sub-options.

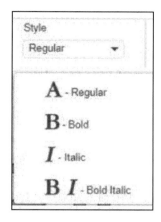

The Regular is the default style of your design canvas. Bold makes your chosen font appear thicker. Italic makes your chosen font tilt to the right while Bold italic makes the italic font thicker.

Font Size, Letter Space, and Line Space.

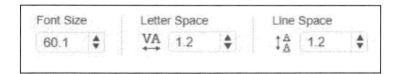

These three options are very amazing as it brings a sort of perfection to your projects.

- <u>Font Size</u>: You can change the size of your text in the Font Size area.

- <u>Letter Space</u>: While some fonts have a considerable space between the letters others don't really have. The letter space option allows you manage the spacing between letters.

- <u>Line Space</u>: This option allows you manage the space between the text lines in a paragraph.

- <u>Alignment</u>: Don't get confused, this particular alignment is different from the other alignment explained initially. This alignment option work with paragraphs.

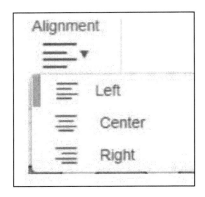

The Alignment option has other sub-options:

- <u>Left</u>: This action aligns selected paragraph(s) to the left.

- <u>Center</u>: This aligns selected paragraph(s) to the center.

- <u>Right</u>: This aligns selected paragraph(s) to the right.

<u>Curve</u>: Do you want to make your text shaped, this option is your best bet. The Curve option allows you make your texts curved.

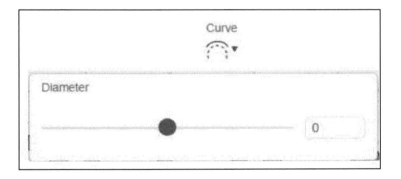

By moving the slider right or left it curves your texts upward or inward.

Advance. Don't get scared about this option, it is as easy as other options. Even though as a beginner you may not use it often, but once you get a hang of it, you are good to go.

Design Space Canvas (Design Panel, Header, Zoom)

<u>A Canvas on Cricut Design Space</u>

Canvas has long been associated with Art — oil painting in particular. Now, there's a new type of Art creation on the scene — Cricut Design Space! And their claiming the name too.

When you push "Canvas" on your menu, it will take you to your new canvas, your workspace.

We'll go over the different parts of your Canvas, now, piece by piece.

<u>Header</u>

The first thing we'll talk about is the Header. It's the black strip you see across the top of the screen.

This image is merely for reference. I'll zoom in as we go over each portion of the Header.

You may be wondering why we're even bothering with the Header, and I almost didn't, but it is important.

We'll go through the parts of the Header from left to right. Some of the parts have already been explained. Others are pretty self-explanatory, but you need to know where the things on here are—and especially that the "Save" button is there!

Menu

This is pretty simple to figure out. The menu for the Canvas area is set up identical to the menu on the Homepage.

Canvas

Pictured above, "Canvas" merely tells you that you are on the Canvas screen.

Title

The title of the project is important. If you're working on more than one project at a time, which I don't recommend, then switching pack and forth would become very frustrating if the title wasn't displayed.

This title also lets me know that, "Hey! This hasn't been saved yet!"

My Projects

"My Projects" on the Canvas page works exactly like the "My Projects" button on the Homepage. The thing you do need to know, though, is that if you click this part of the Header without saving your project first, you will lose your recent changes.

Save

This is the most important part of the Header. So many people don't save enough. Now, it doesn't matter as much in these days as it did long ago when everything relied strictly on the electricity it drew from the wall. If you lose power with a laptop in your lap, it's not as big of a deal.

However, my computer hates me at times. It throws hissy fits. And I know other people who have the same problem. It kicks me out of programs and sometimes even kicks me off the WIFI when no one else is having trouble. That's what you have to worry about. And with Cricut being web-based, if you're on your computer and lose power, which means losing WIFI, you might lose all that hard work too.

Although you probably would have no problem identifying the word, "Save," on the Header, I said I'd give you a picture. Here you go:

Explore

Explore changes which machine you're sending your project to. When you click the down arrow, it gives you a drop-box with the machines listed.

Make It

Once you finish your creation, it's time to print it (if there's any printing involved) and cut it. This is what the "Make It" button is for. It's the only one that actually looks like a button.

Design Panel

On the top right, you'll see a plus sign with a circle around it for starting a new project. We'll be first talking about the vertical taskbar that that's a part of. It's called the Design Panel.

New

Click this to begin a new project. You're already in "New Project" right now, so there's no need to click it at the moment. This is to use later when you're finishing up another project and need to go on to a new one.

Templates

"Templates" is a collection of 2-D pictures of objects such as clothing, bowls, file folders, banners, and more.

However, these are different. They are not for adding to your project, but for adding your project too. They're there for reference.

For instance, if I were to click on the apron, it would throw an apron template up on my canvas for reference only. It would neither save with nor be printed or cut with my project, but it lets me see how large or small I want to make my wording or image.

Projects

This button takes you to the library of ready-to-make projects.

Images

Here, you can insert images. Clicking the images tab on the Design Panel opens an area of images similar to the area of "Projects."

You merely select the image you want and click "Insert Image" in the bottom, right-hand corner of the screen.

If you're having a difficult time finding an image you want, or, on the contrary, you're finding all the images you want, but they all cost more than you wish to pay, you can narrow down your search by enforcing filters.

There are several types of filters you can put into place, and you can check one box or several boxes beside different filters at one time.

Filters are divided into two categories. One category encompasses the images that you have a right to (what you've uploaded, bought, own, made, or what is free). The second category is a breakdown of the types of images you can choose from.

If you still can't find what you want, you can browse the categories or cartridges or do a search for a specific image.

Browse by Category

To kick it off, there is a line of three featured cards. I'm not sure if you can read them in the screenshot. The featured categories are "Free this Week," "Most Popular," and "Recently Added."

The other thirty-six categories include things like:

• Animals & Wildlife

• Baby

• Education & Kids Crafts

• Patriotic

• Spiritual & Religion

• Sports & Recreation

• A Separate Category for Many Special Days and Many Holidays

• And More!

There are also an additional twenty-six categories of Brands.

A few of the brands they offer categories for are:

• Creative Bug

• Martha Stewart

• Marvel

• Sesame Street

• Star Wars

• Vintage Revivals

NOTE: You can also implement your filters inside the categories.

Browse by Cartridge

You can browse by "Cartridge." The difference between browsing categories and cartridges is that when you purchase an image through categories, you're purchasing one image. However, when you purchase a cartridge, you're purchasing a bundle of images.

You can also use your filters in here. And there are plenty of free cartridges as well.

Search for an Image

If you already know what you want an image of, whether it be a dog or cat, a flower, or the words "Kindness Squad," just describe your ideal image in the search bar with as few words as possible.

Here, you can see that I also used the "Free" filter so I could get a "Kindness Squad" image that cost me zero cents.

When you're ready to insert the image, just click on it, as I showed you above. Then click "Insert Image." Cricut Design Space will insert the image onto your canvas, and you can manipulate it from there to make it the size you want it.

If you're using a template, you can click and drag the image on top of the template before you begin sizing it. You click and drag images in Cricut Design Space the same way as you do in any other mainstream computer program. You size it by dragging the bottom, right corner until you get the image the size you want it.

The X in the top left corner will delete the image if you click it. The Round arrow in the upper right will allow you to turn the image. The padlock in the bottom left will lock the image's size and position (as far as what angle it's on. It's position on the canvas doesn't matter. That's just your workspace).

These same principles apply to working with text.

Below is a screenshot of the "Kindness Squad" image set in place and sized on my apron template. Anytime you click the canvas away from the image or text you're working on, the image or text will become inactive. To work with it again, merely click it once more.

Text

When you click on "Text," it brings up a textbox that allows you to type right onto the canvas. As you type the words, they'll appear as a script on your canvas as well.

Text Edit Bar

Because we're in the middle of the Design Panel Section, I should be moving on to the next part on the Design Panel, which is the "Shapes," but I've never been one for following directions. And when I move on from the Design Panel, the next thing I should cover should be the Edit Bar, since it sits on top of the Text Edit Bar at the top of the Canvas. But, again, I'm a rebel. We're going to squeeze in the Text Edit Bar real quick so I can tell you how to edit this text that we just inserted onto the canvas.

This image is for reference only. I'll zoom in on the separate parts for better viewing as we talk about them.

The Text Edit Bar appears and disappears when you click or unclick the text you're working on in Cricut Design Space.

Choosing Your Font

Once you insert your word, phrase, or sentence, you're going to want to select your font.

This might look nice and easy to navigate, and it is, but it's nothing like Microsoft Word's or Word 365's font choices. When you hit down on this, you're given an amazing array of choices. And the options are provided to you with real-life examples.

You can look through "All" the fonts, as you see "All" is chosen among the three choices at the top, center of the "Fonts" box. You can also look through only the fonts on your computer system by clicking "System." Those even look pretty on the Cricut.

You can also single out the Cricut fonts specifically with the next word over.

Next, you see the search box. If you know what font you're looking for, Cricut Design Space makes life easy for you by giving you a way to look it up so you can get it searched, selected, and situated.

Lastly, I wanted to point out that "Text" also has a "Filter" option on it.

Now, there is so much more you can do with Fonts in Cricut Design Space, that's all we'll get into for now.

Back to the Design Panel.

Shapes

The "Shapes" option will add any of the eight Elementary 2-D shapes to your canvas.

NOTE: You, of course, can make your oval and rectangle by stretching your square and circle.

To enter a shape onto your canvas, merely click it. Cricut Design Space will place it onto your canvas for you.

You can then click it and drag it where you want it to go, exactly as I taught you to do with the images and text. You can also size the shapes in the same way as images and text are sized,

Edit Bar

Pardon the interruption to the "Design Panel" once more. I realize we still have one more option to talk about there, that being "Upload." But I want to pause to go over the

"Edit Bar."

The Edit Bar, like the Text Bar, is only available when images or shapes are clicked and, therefore, editable. Otherwise, the Edit Bar is unnecessarily wasted space.

This image is for reference only. I'll zoom in on the separate parts for better viewing as we talk about them.

Undo/Redo Buttons

Ahh... Those handy Undo/Redo Buttons. Don't you hate to make a mistake and then find yourself stuck with no way to fix it? Cricut gives you an undo option! And if that's not good enough, pushing "ctrl" and "z" together will do the same thing—erase those pesky mistakes!

Linetype and Fill

The next two parts of the Edit Bar are the "Linetype" and "Fill." Lintype has three options in its dropdown box. Those options are "Cut," "Draw," and "Score." All this does is change what your Cricut does with your image, text, or shape.

Cut

Linetype is automatically set to "Cut." If you choose "Cut," your machine will merely cuts out whatever shape you have it to cut. This option will also allow you to Print and Cut.

You can choose the color of the material you will be cutting as well. You do this by clicking the colored square beside "Cut" that is currently black.

You can choose any of the colors listed. If you don't see the exact color of your material, you can click the "Advanced" option under the color swatches. "Advanced" will drop-down a big square, which you can use to fine-tune a color.

First, you'll choose the color you want to begin with from the swatches (small colored squares full of color) above the big square. At that time, a small circle will appear in the center of the big square, which will now be the color you chose. You can move the little circle to make it a different color since the colors inside the big square vary slightly as they move away from the little circle (which is the original color on the spectrum).

There is also a slider bar to the right of the big box. The slider will allow you to slowly add the closest primary colors to the current color, making it a different color. For instance, you can make a blue greener by moving the slider downward toward the yellow. As you move the slider, the color in the big color box will change to show you the result.

The "Advanced Color" you're creating will display on the image or text you're changing the cut color on. Therefore, you can watch that to see what color you're creating as you go.

Beside the color box, while the "Linefill" option is on "Cut," you'll see "No Fill" and a diagonal line through the next box over. When you click on the "No Fill" box, there is a dropdown menu with a "Print" option. The "Print" option will give you the option to print the item first that you choose for printing rather than simply cutting it.

If you click "Print," you can choose to have it filled with a color or a pattern. I have "Pattern" chosen in the drop-box seen above. I also included a screenshot of our ongoing image with a pattern below.

The "Color" option under "Print" also has the Advanced options with the big color box and the color slider as well.

Draw

With the "Draw" option will, you will use your Pen accessory on your Cricut. With the Pen located into the Cricut, it will draw whatever you want to be drawn.

After you choose "Draw," you'll move over next to it to the square and click on it. It will give another dropdown menu. In that menu, you'll first choose what type of pen you'll be using.

There are seven types of pens:

• Fine (0.4 mm)

• Extra Fine (0.3 mm)

• Gel (1 mm)

• Glitter Gel (0.8 mm)

• Marker (1 mm)

• Calligraphy (2 mm)

• Calligraphy (2.5 mm)

Your color options will change depending on which type of pen you choose. This is because there are only certain colors available with each pen type.

JUST A NOTE: Some people might try to tell you that you don't have to use a Cricut pen. I've heard people say that a fine or extra fine permanent marker works just as well. And it might. I don't know. What I do know is that using anything in your Cricut machine that's not Cricut produced will void your warranty. Don't do it.

Score

"Score" is for when you want to create a crease line for easy folding.

Select All

It's so much easier to have a "Select All" button than to have to draw a box around every single thing on your canvas. Cricut Design Space heard their crafters' voices as they said so and made sure to make "Select All" possible.

The below box shows both "Edit" and "Select All." You only have to click the "Select All" to have all of your images and text effortlessly selected!

If you don't feel like clicking the option, you can also just hit "ctrl" and "z" on your PC.

Edit

With "Edit," pictured above, you can "Cut" a selected image or text, which erases from your Canvas (remember, if you didn't mean to Cut it, merely click the "Undo" arrow).

"Copy" will copy the selected item, and "Paste" will paste it elsewhere. After, it's so much easier to copy and paste than it is to find and insert the same image or text twice!

229

Also, if you need to copy and paste multiple items, you can select multiple items at once. Click "Copy." Click "Paste." Now, all you have to do is drag each individual item where you want it. This saves you from having to copy and paste multiple times.

If you have a PC, then you can use these controls: "Ctrl" and "c," pressed together, will also copy your item(s). You can press "ctrl" and "v" to paste them. And, lastly, "ctrl" and "x" will do the same thing as clicking "Cut."

If you have a Mac, the controls are the same, but you will use the command key.

Using Images In Design Space

There are more than 50,000 images in the Cricut Library. With the Design space, you have permission to try these images for free in order to confirm its suitability in your desired project or projects and then after that you can purchase it.

So, how do you use images in Cricut Design Space? Here are simple steps on how to use images in your project:

1. Create a new project by signing in to your Design Space

2. Click on Images located at the left hand side of the design screen if you are using Windows/Mac computer or tap on Image button situated at the bottom left corner of the design screen if you are using iOS/Android device.

You can also browse, filter and search the images in order to choose the ones you intend to use in your project:

I. All Images—use this option to search for a particular image in your Cricut Library or even view featured images

II. Categories—use this option is more like filter tool. It is used to browse images by selecting any one of the image categories.

III.   Cartridges—use this option to search through the list of 400+ Cricut cartridges alphabetically or even search for a specific one.

3. Insert the desired image(s) into your project

4. Edit the images as much as you like.

How to Print Then Cut Using Your Cricut Machine

The first thing to do when you want to achieve this is to first start with your Cricut Design Space. So, let's go there:

Step One: Cricut Design Space

First of all, you know that you can access the Cricut Design Space using your regular internet devices. Right? Good. It doesn't matter the Operating System used by that device because a lot of these devices are compatible with the Cricut Design Space program.

It is widely known that majority of our regular internet devices use either Windows OS, Mac OS, Android OS or iOS. You don't have any problem what OS that you have on your device as we will discuss how to upload or place an image unto the Canvas of the Cricut Design Space using each of these OS. By this, no one is left behind.

First, let us start with the Windows/Mac OS on a laptop/notebook.

On Windows/Mac

The first thing to do is to open your Cricut Design Space which will show the canvas area as displayed below

1. Choose Upload on the design panel which you can located at the bottom left of the Canvas.

You can drag and drop the file you intend to use unto the upload window or you can select browse to locate your desired file from your compute.

2. Remember that you can upload Basic Image or Vector Image. For now, we will not bother ourselves with the technicalities of these images. What we want to achieve is to get an image unto the canvas using the options below:

• Select and then open your desired image file or you can drag and drop the file unto the canvas. As you know, there are over 50,000 images you can play with in the Cricut Design Space library and the number will increase with your own customized images on your computer.

• From the screen, choose what best describes your desired image type. It can be simple, moderately complex or complex

• Click Continue

• Do you have unwanted background in the image you intend to edit? If so, then you need to define the cut lines of your image using Select & Erase. You can also use Erase and Crop. When you have removed the unwanted background, move to the next option.

• Select the Preview to view the cut lines of your image. The essence of this option is to find out if you are okay with the image you want to print and if you are not satisfied with the preview, you can hide the preview to edit your image again.

• If you are satisfied with the image, select Continue.

• Give your image a name and tag it.

• Select Save. To ensure that your image save properly, click on Print and Cut before clicking on Save button because if you click on only Cut, your image will not save properly and you may have to upload it all over again. Am sure you don't want that to happen.

3. After saving, the image will be uploaded into your uploaded images.

4. Select the image and insert it into the Canvas.

5. Resize it to suit your desired project.

6. Click Make It. Your image will be shown with a black bounded box.

7. Select Continue.

So, you have finished your first step with the Cricut Design Space and you now ready to print. Jump to the Print Section to continue the steps.

On Android device:

If you have an Android device, then follow the steps below to place an image unto the Canvas. The picture below is an open blank Canvas on Android device.

1. Tap the Upload tool located at the bottom of the screen as shown above.

2.You can decide to take a photo, select from the photo library or open an uploaded image.

3. If you desire to "Select from Photo Library" from your file storage application where the image is saved, then tap to select an image and open it. You may have to clean your image if there are unwanted backgrounds or any addition to it.

4. Click Done when you have finish cleaning the image to your satisfaction.

5. Tap Next at the upper right corner of the screen.

6. You need to name your image and choose how you desire to save it.

7. Your Uploaded images library will open next where you can select the image to insert unto the Canvas.

8. After saving the image will be uploaded into your uploaded images.

9. Select the image and insert it into the Canvas.
10. Resize it to suit your desired project.
11. Click Make It.Your image will be shown with a black bounded box.
12. Select Continue.

Next, jump to the Print section to continue.

On iOS device:

What if you are using an iOS device, then follow the steps below to upload or select your desired image unto the Canvas. An empty Canvas on iOS device is shown below

1. Locate the Upload tool at the bottom of the screen and tap it.

2. Tap on the Browse files to search for your desired image or file from the available storage applications in your device.

3. Clean up the image and define its cut lines using the edit tools as in Windows/Mac OS.

4. Select Next button located at the upper right corner of your screen

5. Make final adjustments to your image using the Refine screen before you saving it to your library.

6. Tap Next

7. Choose how you want to save your final image; either as Cut image or Print Then Save.

8. Tap on the Save button located at the upper right corner of your screen.

9. When your Uploaded Images library opens, select the desired image you intend to upload unto the Canvas.
10. After saving, the image will be uploaded into your uploaded images.

11. Select the image and insert it into the Canvas.

12. Resize it to suit your desired project.

13. Click Make It. Your image will be shown with a black bounded box.

14. Select Continue.

Next, jump to the Print Section to continue.

Print

In order to print your image with the printer,

1. Select Send to Printer. Ensure that your image is saving to your preferred printer after clicking Send to Printer

2. Select Print.

And boom! Your image is printed for you.

Cut

1. Align the printed copy to the top left corner of the mat with the image facing upward.

2. Load it unto your Cricut machine with the image facing upward too.

3. Set the type of material from your Cricut Design space.

4. Ensure you have your fine point blade in place.

5. Turn fast mode On.

6. Click on the Load button and flashing Cricut button to load and cut your image respectively for you.

7. When done, press the Unload button and remove your mat from the Cricut machine.

8. Remove your cut image and place on your desired object including mugs, wine glasses, etc. Some of these projects are displayed below.

How to work with uploaded photos and edit images

Have you tried to find out how to edit pictures in the layout room of Cricut? Also me. Usually, I leave Cricut Design Space to do my edits on another program and then return the altered picture to Cricut Design Space. But there's no more! I lastly found out the tricks in Cricut Design Space to edit images.

Editing Images In Cricut Design Space Using The Slice Tool

To assist me in editing pictures in the Cricut Design Space, I used the Slice device. I'm likely still going to use that method for photos I've already uploaded to Cricut Design Space. Let me explain how to edit images using the Slice tool.

1. Click on the picture and then click Insert Images to add your attached picture to your Cricut Design Space canvas. You can add more than one image to your canvas at a time.

2. Make your picture a lot larger so you can work on it by pressing and pulling it down a little bit on the right upper corner. Just far enough to be able to see it better.

3. I want to get rid of the dog in the image I've uploaded. I don't see any canvas wiping alternative, so I'm trying to use the Slice tool to cut the dog out. In the left-hand toolbox, press Shapes, then press the circle.

4. Unlock the table by pressing below the square on the left upper panel. Do you see the icon of the lock? Click on that. Now, using the right top corner, you can transfer the square in any form you want. I placed the circle over the portion that I was about to wipe out, the dog.

5. Clicking or highlighting the circle, click and hold the change key on your keyboard. Click the picture of the bubble with your mouse, well, bubble for me. This emphasizes both of them.

6. Click the Slice device at the right upper corner with both the circle and the picture outlined.

7. Start taking back your slice's parts. There ought to be three parts. They can be deleted.

8. Continue this method until the manner you want your picture to be printed.

Editing images in the design space of Cricut when uploading images

1. For this method to operate, you will need to upload a picture from your desktop. Click complicated once you upload it, and the next window is where the magic takes place.

2. At the left corner of the top. Look at the wand? Click on it and press on the hair. Click on the continuation button and name the picture. Click the save button.

It's gone, and it's been so simple. Now, let's look after her flesh.

3. I gotta upload her again. I'm going to operate on erasing the corpse this moment. First press back on the magic wand to remove the face, arms, body, and any hard-to-reach pieces. Once you've finished that, take the eraser to wash the remainder of your flesh until it's gone.

Click Continue, identify your picture, and then press Save when the image is to your liking.

Insert both pictures into the surface of your Cricut Design Space. You can bring them back together once you've got them there. One reason I'm excited about this process is that sometimes, like the hair colour, I want to change things. I couldn't change the hair colour if I left the picture like it was. But I can do that now.

Would you like to know how to edit images in Cricut Design Space as thrilled as I am? I pray so.

Now, go out and do some crafting!

The Knockout Text Method

Until recently, I hadn't heard of "knockout" writing, but I decided to try it out once I saw models using this method! Knockout text is a technique you use to shape a portion of your message using a picture. Usually, the abbreviation "Impact" is used in the technique of knockout.

This method basically utilizes the Slice and Weld tool to produce these fantastic patterns in a slightly distinct manner.

How to Do Knockout Text in Cricut Design Space

First, in the drop-down Font panel, you will enter your name and select the font, "Impact." The Slice instrument only operates with 2 layers in order to produce a single layer; you need to Weld your text together.

Ungroup your writing and bring it all nearer together. (If you don't want to unbundle them, you can also use the Letter Space device). The knockout display is based on your picture as a portion of your writing, and you will lose the knockout impact if the text is spread out too much. You can use the Align tool to completely tag up and centre your writing after you have your letters spaced as you want them. Click on the Weld instrument to select all of your content.

Only one part continues after the text has been welded as in the picture below. You are now prepared to attach a photo

Select Insert Pictures and find "Witch." Insert your layout display with the witch picture. In the Layers section, click the circle next to your image and alter the colour to green to make it simpler to see. Remember, the impact of knockout is to display the image only where you have text. Any portion of the non-text image will subsequently be removed. So shape your image to contain most of it in your text. The moon is totally out of the text in the instance below, so it will be removed subsequently.

Now that you've lined up your picture, you're supposed to pick your text layer and picture layer and tap on the Design Screen's Slice instrument at the top left.

On the Layers panel, you will now see the cut picture and additional layers. Your photo or text should NOT be moved. You need to remain lined up with them. You want any part of the image that is not in the book to be deleted. On the Layers menu, this is simplest to do.

Once you have removed your additional layers, you will have only two layers left which is what you want to pull out. You can also see that the script only keeps your picture inside and shapes the text. This is the technique of knockouts.

Repeat the above measures individually with each picture to add the moon and bat. This will sound like your completed layout:

Okay, quite simple? Using this method for a fun shirt or even pillow patterns is enjoyable. In the knockout technique on the Cricut page, you can see another way to do various stages.

Advanced Tips And Tricks

Learning to use the "Cricut" machine definitely involves a steep learning curve. The more complicated aspect of it all is using the "Design Space" software to hone down a variety of features and tools to help you craft your designs and turn your "inspiration into creation". There are multiple shortcuts on the "Design Space" application to make your designing not only easy but more efficient. Let's look at some of the tips and tricks that will make your creative self-stronger and happier!

"Design Space" application

• The "Weld", "Contour" and "Slice" functionalities to customize your designs. These 3 tools will be activated at the bottom of the screen for designs that allow for these changes.

• The "Weld" tool will allow you to merge two different designs to obtain one composite design, without any leftover seams and cut lines that might be present on the individual designs. This helps you in obtaining single continuous cut for your design so you do not need to glue and assemble multiple pieces to obtain the final design, for example, creation of cake toppers, gift tags and other decorations.

• The "Contour" tool can be used to activate or deactivate any cut lines in any cut files and thereby allowing you to customize the image in various ways. So imagine you have an image of a flower and you want to remove the details of the design and obtain more of an outline of the flower, you can do so by clicking on the "Contour" button at the bottom of the screen and selecting the different elements of the image that you want to turn on or off from the contour pop-up window.

• The "Slice" tool can be used to slice a design from an image by cutting out or removing elements of the image, as shown in the picture below.

• Use your search keywords wisely. The search functionality within the "Design Space" is not very dynamic so your choice of keywords will make a big difference on the designs and projects that will be displayed to you. For example, if you search for images containing dotted designs and search with keyword "Dots", you would be given around 120 images but if you search with the term "Dot" you would see almost twice as many images. You should also search with synonyms and closely related terms of your target project idea. For instance, if you wanted to create a Halloween project, you can search with terms like pumpkin, costumes and trick or treat among others. This will ensure you are viewing any and all images pertaining to your project.

• The "Cartridge" image sets. It is likely that during your search, you like a design more than any other made available to you but it is not exactly how you want it to be. Well, simply click on the small information circle (i) at the bottom of the image and you will be able to view the entire image set or "cartridge" of images similar to your selected image within the "Design Space Image Library".

• A treasure trove of free fonts and images. As a beginner you would want to utilize a large number of free fonts and images to get your hands-on experience with your "Cricut" device. This is a great way to spend less money and still be able to create stunning craft projects. Within the "Design Space" application, you can click on the "Filter" icon next to the search bar (available within the images, fonts and projects tabs) and select "Free" to only view free resources within each category.

• Use synchronized colors to save time and money. This is a great tool when you have designs that are either a composite of multiple images or inherently contains different hues of the same color. Instead of using 5 different shades of the same color, you can synchronize the colors so you need to use only one colored sheet. To do this, simply click on the "Color Sync" tab on the "Layers Panel" on the top right corner of the screen. Then drag and drop desired layer(s) of the design to your target color layer and the moved layer will immediately be modified to have the same color as the target color.

• Use the "Hide" tool to selectively cut images from the Canvas. When you are looking to turn your imagination into a work of art, you may want to view and take inspirations from multiple images while you work on your design. But once you obtain your desired design you would not want to cut every other image on your canvas. This is where the "Hide" tool comes in handy, so you do not need to delete the images on the Canvas to avoid cutting them along with your project design. To hide the image, you just need to click on the "eye" symbol next to those specific image layers on the "Layers Panel". The hidden images will not be deleted from the Canvas but would not appear on the cutting mat when you click the "Make It" button to cut your project.

• Ability to change the design lines to be cut, scored or drawn. With the latest version of the "Design Space" application, you have the ability to simply change the "Linetype" of a design from its predefined type to your desired action, instead of looking for designs that have predefined line type meeting your project need. For example, if your selected design is set at "Linetype" Cut but you want the design to be "Linetype" Score, you can easily change the "Linetype" by clicking on the "Linetype" drop-down and making your selection.

• The power of the "Pattern" tool. You can use your own uploaded images to be used as pattern fill for your designs. Moreover, you will also be able to edit the image pattern and the patterns that already exist within the "Design Space" application to create your own unique and customized patterns. The "Edit Pattern" window allows you to adjust the resolution and positioning of the pattern on your design and much more. (Remember, to use the "Pattern" feature you must use the "Print then Cut" approach for your project, with access to a printer).

• Utilize the standard "keyboard shortcuts". The "Design Space" application does have all the required tools and buttons to allow you to edit the images and fonts but if you prefer to use your keyboard shortcuts to quickly edit the image, the "Design Space" application will support that. Some of the keyboard shortcuts you can use include: "Copy (Control + C)"; "Paste (Control + V)"; "Delete (Delete key)"; "Copy (Control + Z)".

• You can utilize the "Slice" tool to crop the image. The "Design Space" application still lacks the "Crop" functionality, so if you need to crop an image, you will need to get creative. A good tip is to use the "Slice" tool along with the "Shapes" to get your desired image.

• Change the position of the design on the cutting Mat. When you are ready to cut your design and click on the "Make It" button, you will notice that your design will be aligned on the top left corner of the mat. Now, if you are using material that was priorly cut at its top left corner, you can simply drag and move the image on the "Design Space" mat to meet the positioning of your cutting material. You will be able to cut the image anywhere on the mat by moving the design on that specific position on the mat.

• Moving design from one mat to the another. Yes! You can not only move the design over the mat itself, you can also move the design from one mat to another by simply clicking on the three dots (...) on top of the mat and select "Move to another mat". You will then view a pop-up window where you can select from the existing mats for your project to be used as the new mat for your selected design.

• Save cut materials as Favorites for quick access. Instead of spending time filtering and searching for your cut material on the "Design Space" application over and over, just save your frequently used material by clicking on the star next to the "Cricut" logo on the "Design Space" application to save them under the "Favorites" tab next to the default "All Materials" tab. When you are getting ready to cut your project, under the "Set

Material" tab, your "Favorites" material will be displayed on the screen, as shown in the picture below.

• You can store the most frequently used cut materials on the "Cricut Maker". Unlike the "Cricut Explore" series which has dial settings for a variety of commonly used cut materials, the "Cricut Maker" requires you to use a "Custom Materials" menu within the "Design Space" application that can be accessed using the button on the machine bearing "Cricut" logo, since there is no dial to choose the material you want to cut.

• Choose to repeat the cut of the same mat or skip a mat from being cut altogether. By following the instructions on the "Design Space" and feeding the right color and size of the material to the machine, you will be able to get your design perfectly cut. You can change the order in which the mats are cut, repeat the cut of your desired mat and even skip cutting a mat, if needed. You can do this easily by simply clicking on and selecting the mat you would like to cut.

• You can edit the cut settings your materials. You might notice that even when you have selected the default settings to cut the desired material, the material may not cut as desired. To help with this, "Design Space" allows you to adjust the cut settings for all the materials such as the depth of the cut, the cutting blade and the number of the passes to be made by the "Cricut" device. Since this may not be as intuitive to most beginners, here's a step by step walkthrough of this process:

1. When using the "Cricut Maker", select "Materials" on the cut screen and if using the "Cricut Explore" series, set the dial to "Custom".

2. Click on "Browse All Materials" from the top of the menu.

3. From the bottom of the screen, select "Material Settings".

4. The pop-up window for the "Custom Materials" will be displayed as shown in the picture below, where you can make the required adjustments.

• Adjust the pressure with which the material can be cut. You may want to just adjust the pressure with which the cut is made to obtain clean and neat cut of the material, without needing to going through the process described above to adjust the cut setting of the material. On the cut screen, once you have selected the cut material, a drop-down option with "Default" setting will be displayed. Simply click on the drop-down button, and adjust pressure to "More" or "Less".

• "Cricut Access Membership" – At a monthly fee of around $8 or an annual membership fee, you will be able to use a larger variety of fonts and imaged for free. You will be able to freely use more than 30K images, over 370 fonts and thousands of projects saving a lot of money in the long run, depending on your usage.

<u>"Cricut" devices, tools and accessories</u>

• How to clean your cutting mat - If you would like to prolong the life of your cutting mats, it is important to clean them every now and then (if not after each use). You can just wipe the mat with baby wipes or use other wet wipes that do not contain any alcohol and are fragrance free. This will ensure that there is not residual build up from cardstock and vinyl and other such materials and from accumulating dust and lint.

• Carry out a sample cut prior to cutting your design – To make sure that you do not end up with a cut that does not meet your expectations it is recommended to do a test cut first. This will help you check the sharpness of the blade as well as the cut setting for your material and make the required adjustments to get clean cut projects.

• Carefully remove the materials off the cutting mat – It is highly recommended to use appropriate tools to remove the material from the mat. But it is equally important to pay attention to how you are peeling the design from the mat. To prevent the material from getting damaged, it is better to peel the mat away from the design by turning the mat upside down and bending a corner of the material. Then you can slip in the spatula to remove the project easily and with no damage.

• Use "Non-Cricut" craft pen(s) – If you have Sharpie pens or other craft pens, don't be afraid to use them with your "Cricut" device to save some money from buying new pen.

• Dedicated blades to increase the shelf life - If you are able to use dedicated bladed for your frequently used cutting material, your blades will last longer. For instance, you can have one blade for vinyl only and another just to cut cardstock. Since both the materials, in this case, have different strength, the pressure and sharpness required to produce clean cut will also vary. Therefore, dedicated blades will maintain it's sharpness much longer.

• Storage of mats and vinyl rolls – Using standard hooks, you can easily hang your mats as a display on the wall. This will make the mats more accessible and you would not need to spend time searching for the required mats. Similarly, you can utilize trash bag holders to store and organize your vinyl or paper rolls and easily retrieve the desired material when needed.

• No "BrightPad"! No Problem! – It is definitely ideal to weed your vinyl and other delicate designs by placing the design on top of the "BrightPad. The light from the "BrightPad" peeks through the cut lines so you can easily weed the design without damaging it. But if you do not want to invest in a "BrightPad", try hanging the vinyl on a window for similar light effect to carefully weed your design.

• Convenient Charging Port – The "Cricut Maker" device is equipped with USB port on the side that will allow you to power your electronic devices, so you can charge your phone or tablet while you work to get your craft projects completed.

• Tips when working with wood – The wood projects tend to be time consuming and labor intensive and of course, long lasting. So, you want to get it right the first time. Below are some tips to help you get the best wood projects with no stress.

• Ensure that your projects are carried out using a sealer so that the wood does not get damaged unexpectedly.

• When using vinyl or iron-on designs, use sanding paper to sand the wood and obtain a flat surface prior to application of the design. Wooden plaques are not always flat, as it's a natural product. The surface may need to be sand so that all sections of the design material will stick evenly on the surface.

• Consider using a stamping effect for your paper design, when using wood and paper designs to produce a rustic feel for your project.

• When choosing a stain color for the wooden plaque, make sure that your project color aligns with that color and other project that you already have in your house. Don't be scared to combine different wood stain colors and use your own customized stain!

• For easy and effective application of wood glue, it is recommended to wet the wood with a damp cloth first. After the wood glue has been applied to the plaque, clamp it and allow it to set for at least 24 hours.

• If you are planning to use pallet wood make sure to clean the pallet plaque using a wire brush.

How To Use Design Space On Mobile Device

How to Install/Uninstall Design Space

Let us tackle how to install/uninstall on these platforms including Windows, Mac, iOS and android devices.

Install on Windows/Mac:

• Click on your browser and navigate to www.design.cricut.com

• If you are a first time user, you need to create a Cricut ID otherwise sign in with your Cricut ID. Ensure that the page is fully loaded before carrying out this activity in order to avoid error.

• Select New Project.

• Select Download Plugin from the prompt.

• Wait for the download to finish and then select the downloaded file to Open/Run it.

• Click Next when the Cricut installer opens.

• Read the Terms of Use and accept the agreement.

• Click Install to begin installation

• Click Done at the end of the installation.

Install Cricut Design Space App on iOS

• Tap on the App Store icon on your device

• Search for Cricut Design Space

• Tap the Get button to download. Please confirm the download with your iTunes password if prompted. The app will launch and display the necessary options that will used to complete the process.

Install Cricut Design Space App on Android

• Tap Google Play Store App on your device to open it

• Search for Cricut Design Space

• Tap on the Install button

• Tap on the Cricut Design Space icon to open it when the installation is complete

• Sign in and start designing your project

Uninstall the Cricut Design Space on iOS

• Press and hold the Design Space icon on your iOS device till it vibrates

• Press the X button to delete it from your device. This is very easy right?

Uninstall Cricut Design Space App on Android

•Go to Settings

•Tap on "Apps" or "Applications"

• Swipe to the "Download" tab or "Application Manager"

• Search for the App you intend to uninstall

• Tap "Uninstall" button to finish and the App is gone for good.

Uninstall on Mac

• Move to Finder and open the Applications folder

• Search for Cricut Design Space

• Drag it to trash

• Right click on the Trashcan and select Empty Trash to remove the Application

Uninstall on Windows

• Click on the Start button.

• Select Settings

• Select Application

- Look for Cricut Design Space and choose Uninstall

How to center your designs to cut in Cricut Design Space

- Sign in to the Cricut Design section. Click on the new project.

- Click Download.

- Click Upload Picture.

- Click Browse.

- Save your picture

- Select the saved image and insert an image.

- Select the picture. Click on it.

- As you can see, the picture is automatically moved to the upper left corner.

- To prevent this, you can fool the software by placing the image in the center of your design area and the mat. This is useful if you want to create openings in the middle of a page.

- Click on the shape tool.

- Create a shape of 11.5 x 11.5 inches.

- Select the square and change the setting to cut it in the drawing.

- The square now appears as an outline.

- Click Align and Center with the selected pattern and square.

- Click the arrow of the size of your square and resize it without moving the top left corner to reduce the size of the square.

- Select the square and pattern, then click Attach. Click on it.

- As you can see now, the design is centered.

How to write with sketch pens in Cricut Design Space

- Sign in to the Cricut Design section. Create a new project.

- Click Download.

- Select upload a picture.

- Click Browse.

- Open your file. Then save To get a good effect, use a file with thin lines and no large spaces.

- Click on the pattern and paste it.

- Select the pattern.

- Change the drawing to a drawing.

- You will now see the drawing as an outline drawn.

- Click on it.

• Your drawing will now be displayed on the cutting screen. Click on Continue.

• If you change your drawing to draw, the software automatically selects the pen tool. Insert the pen or marker into the recommended clip. Insert paper and click on the start icon.

• The pen now draws your pattern.

How to upload PNG file

After you've converted your PDF document to PNG file format, there are some ways to clean up the file before printing and then crop it with Cricut® Design Space.

• Click Create New Project.

• Click Upload Picture.

• Click on the image to upload

• Click Browse

• The Open dialog box opens. Select the PNG file you want to upload and click

• An example of a picture can be found in Cricut® Design Space. Since we want to edit this file, we select Complex Image and click Next

• The PNG file is loaded into Cricut® Design Space. Select and Delete

How to convert a pdf to PNG format

• After downloading the PDF document to your computer, open your browser and go to png2pdf.com.

• Click on the upload files

• The "Open File" dialog box starts. Locate the PDF file to convert (probably in the Downloads folder), click the PDF file and click The file is uploaded. You should see a progress bar. Once the file has been uploaded and converted, a Download button appears below the small image of the uploaded file.

• Click on the download The file is downloaded as a ZIP file and appears in the status bar at the bottom of the screen. Just click on the filename to open the ZIP file.

• The Open File dialog opens, and the downloaded file should be displayed. Since the file is still in ZIP format, you must first unzip or unzip it. Just click Extract All Files.

• The Open File dialog opens, and your newly converted PDF file should be displayed in PNG file. You can open the file with a double-click if you only want to see what the file looks like. Close the window now by clicking on the red X.

• After you have converted your PDF file to PNG format, you must upload the PNG file to Cricut® Design Space so that you can use the Print and Cut functions.

Working with Edit Bar in Cricut Design Space

Here are important terminologies to help our understanding of the Design Space Edit Bar will have to be defined. A word of caution though, is that some of the terms used here are common tools for everyday use on the computer so it shouldn't be difficult to understand but our level of computer literacy is not the same. Therefore, pardon me if you already know many of them. This has been done for the sake of those who do not know. The terms are as follows:

• Undo/Redo - refers to undoing any change made to the layer or redo any priorly taken undone action.

• Linetype - refers to how the machine will interact with the material on the mat including cut, draw and score as described below.

• Cut - refers to cutting layer with the aid of a blade from your material.

• Draw - refers to drawing the layer with the aid of a Cricut pen.

• Score - refers to scoring the layer using a Scoring Stylus or Scoring Wheel.

• Linetype Swatch - refers to choosing additional attributes that your layer will use. There are different types of options you can select from based on the selected Linetype (cut, draw, and score).

Working with Fonts in Design Space

The ability to personalize project with the use of distinct fonts and text is one of the unique features of the Cricut Design Space. Why is this unique? Because it gives you the freedom to express the creativity of your mind. This creative ability is innate in us and there is this satisfaction accompanied by a great sense of accomplishment that is felt whenever the projects are delivered to taste.

The Cricut Design Space has another amazing feature which is the ability to change the font after ungrouping or isolating the letters, you can use the Cricut fonts or the one installed on your computer or device.

How to Select Font

If you have ever worked with Image Edit Tool before, then you will definitely be at home with the Text Edit tool in Cricut Design

Space. This is because the two tools are similar in their mode of operation in rotating, sizing and positioning of text. The similarity of the tools will excite you because it makes the job simpler when editing the text and locating the right font. With this, you can personalize projects easily.

How to Edit Fonts

The Edit bar in Cricut design Space, grants you access to edit the features of particular images or text. These features include Linetype, Size, Rotate, Fill, Position and Mirror. In the Text layers, there are additional options in the Text layers including Line Spacing, font styles and letter spacing. So how do you edit the font? Here, I will show you.

Select the text object you want to edit on the Canvas or you can insert text from design panel, or select a text layer from the Layers Panel. Once it is selected, the Text Edit Bar will pop up directly below Standard Edit Bar. Note that the Standard Edit Bar will be hidden when you are not interacting with the text.

When the Text Edit Bar pops up, you can begin to manipulate the font using the options described below. Simple right?

How to Add Text to Cricut Design Space

Navigate to the left hand side of the Canvas and select the Text tool. When the Text tool is selected, the font list will open if you are using iOS/Android or the Text bar and text box will pop up for users with Windows/Mac.

Select the desired font size and the font type you intend to use and then input your text. If you intend to start on a new line of text on the same textbox, use the 'Return' key after the prior line of text. Do not freak out when you did not choose the font setting before typing the text, with Cricut Design Space, it is possible to type the text before selecting the font on a Windows/Mac computer.

• Click or tap on any area outside the text box to close it.

• To edit the text is pretty simple. Double click on the text to display available options.

• The Edit bar is found at the top of the Canvas for Windows/Mac users and at the bottom of the Canvas for iOS/Android users.

How to Troubleshoot Error codes in the cricut design space

Every electronic device pops up error when there is a conflict with its program. The Cricut Design Space is no exception because it is also a program running on your device and will also complain if something is missing from its chain of command. As a user interface, it will report this error to you for correction in order to complete its current task.

Let us describe some of these errors and how to troubleshoot them. If you still cannot solve the problem after going through these steps or the error is not treated here, please feel free to contact Customer Care.

• Error (0)

Restart your computer and machine.

If your device is short of that then, ensure that your computer or device satisfy these minimum requirements or try to use another computer or device that meet the requirements.

Clear your cache, browser history, cookies and ensure that your browser is updated to the current version.

Recreate the project if only one and not multiple project is affected.

Use another computer or device if the above troubleshooting options fail.

• Error (-11): "Device Authentication" error

Close all background programs on your computer or device and then try again.

Check to see that your browser is updated to the current version.

- Error (-18): "Device Timeout" error

Switch off your computer or device

Close Design Space

restart the Design Space

Power on the Cricut maker and then try to cut again.

If no solution, contact Member Care

- Error (-21): "data transmission" error

Clear your cache, browser history and cookies

Close your browser, re-launch it again and then try cutting

Use a different browser to try cut

Check your internet speed and ensure that it meets the minimum requirement

Contact your Internet Service Provider (ISP) for assistance

- Error (-24): "Ping Timeout" error

Recreate the project because it is possible that the project file is too large or is not properly saved

Try another USB port on the computer or make use of Bluetooth

Use a different USB cable.

Check your internet speed

If nothing works, try a different computer

• Error (-32): Firmware Not Available" error

Since this error pops up only when there is compatibility problem, check the connectivity of your device to the Cricut machine.

if you are 100% sure that the connectivity is correct, then contact Member Care for assistance

• Error (-33): "Invalid Material Setting"

Check the Smart Set Dial. This error appears when there is no selected material from the Design space and the Smart Set Dial is set to "Custom". Therefore, ensure that a material is selected from the Design space material drop down menu.

Try a different material setting.

Contact Member Care for assistance.

FAQ

Where can I download the software for the Explore machines?

You can go to design.cricut.com and use your Cricut ID to log in.
This process is relatively easy and anyone comfortable enough to
download things from the computer will be able to do this. Even
if you have never downloaded anything before, the website will
prompt you to download Design Space and everything after that
will be guided as well.

Where can I download the software if I am on mobile?

If you are on iOS, you have to go to the App Store and search for
the Cricut Design Space app. If you are on Android, simply go to
Google Play and search for the same thing. All you have to do is
download it like any other app, log in, and you are ready to use
Design Space.

What are the differences between the machines?

The Explore One does not have Bluetooth and will need a Cricut
Wireless Bluetooth Adapter to use with your mobile. The Explore
Air, Explore Air 2 and Cricut Maker all have built in Bluetooth.

The explore One also has a single Carriage which means that it cannot multitask like the Explore Air, Explore Air 2 and Cricut Maker.

The Explore Air 2 comes in different colors and cuts faster than the Explore Air and the Explore One.

The Cricut Maker has storage space and can cut through thicker materials.

Does my machine come with a carry bag of sorts?

No, it does not. A carry bag can be purchased from the store but is incredibly overpriced. What's the use of having a Cricut if you can't make your own carry bag?

Writing and scoring, can I do it?

Yes, you can. With the Explore Air, Explore Air 2 and Cricut Maker, you can either write and cut or score and cut at the same time. The Cricut One can do all of it too, but not at the same time.

Is the Design Space the same for both the Cricut Maker and the Explore?

Yes, to my discontent, it is. I am not a fan of Design Space, but I have been told that I am a boomer and do not like it because I can't be bothered to learn it. Long story short; it is exactly the same.

Does the Cricut maker have fast mode?

Yes, it does. It has a setting for up to 2x faster than normal.

What is the thickest my cutting materials can be for the Cricut Explore machines?

The Explore machines can cut materials up to 2mm, but nothing thicker.

What is the thickest my cutting materials can be for the Cricut Maker?

The Cricut Maker can cut materials up to 2.5mm which doesn't sound like much but makes a huge difference.

Do I need the Internet?

Yes and no. When you are on desktop, there is no offline option for Design Space. However, if you are on mobile, the app will allow you to work offline and you won't need the Internet for any of it.

Can Design Space work on more than one device?

Yes. Design Space works with the cloud and not a specific device. This means that anything with access to the cloud can access your account and use your Cricut Machine without any hassle.

How long do images I have purchased stay in my possession?

Images do not expire once you have purchased them. They stay yours forever.

Why is my material tearing all the time and what can I do to stop it?

There are many reasons as to why your materials might be tearing. It could be that you are not using the right settings, your blade is too blunt, the design that you are trying to cut is too intricate and you need to make it larger, or cut slower. There are more possibilities, though. You could be using the wrong blade for your crafts or your materials just aren't working well enough with your Cricut Maker and you might want to invest in better materials next time. Your mat may also be too sticky or too loose.

Are my old blades compatible with the Cricut Maker?

Yes, they are. The Cricut Maker is compatible with old accessories and tools as well as new ones that will be released in the future.

How do I change the blades and accessories?

For the blades you can merely open the clamp marked with a B and remove the blade housing. Now you have an empty clamp and you won't be able to do anything without another blade in the clamp.

To replace the blade in the housing, all you have to do is remove the blade carefully so you don't cut yourself, remove the protective cover from the new blade, and put that in the new housing just like the one you took out. There is a magnet in the housing that keeps the blades in place. All that's left is to return the housing to the clamp and you will be ready to go.

For the accessories you want to open the clamp and slide the accessory adaptor out. Do this by pushing it upward from below. Add your accessory and put it back in the clamp.

The Cricut Explore One only has one clamp which means you will have to switch between the accessory adapter and blade housing. It changes nothing about the process of replacing the blades and accessories. The only difference is that both use the same clamp.

All You Need to Know to Become a Professional Cricut Designer

The scrapbook business has exploded, releasing an ever-increasing number of devices that help you transform your photos into works of art that cement your memories for a lifetime.

As a scrapbooker, there are a couple of instruments that you need to enable you to make the simplest to the most dynamic scrapbook pages you have ever seen. In your basic package, you ought to have devices for journaling, following your photos and components, paper, adornment, and a trimming instrument. As your expertise grows, you can include further developed devices, like the die cutting apparatuses.

The purpose of scrapbooking is to recount a tale about the occasion that prompted the image. Journaling is a component of each page. To journal effectively, you should select markers or pens that are not corrosive. They ought to be quality. Pens and labels come in numerous hues that will make your pages come to life. Make certain to check the tips. A few markers are for shading and are less successful as composing instruments.

Glues. Glues ought to be clean and not corroded. Office tape or paste can harm your photographs and yellow your pages. A tape sprinter would be an amazing basic instrument for a beginning scrapbooker. Tape sprinters can be refilled or discarded. You should check that your tape sprinter can accompany strips, dabs or more extensive groups. Your tape sprinter could likewise accompany a lasting or repositionable glue. If you are experimenting with your page, use repositionable glue. If you are content with your plan, use lasting glue. For experienced scrapbookers, you can get cement machines that will transform paper or other slim materials into stickers. Glue gadgets can work with things from one inch wide up to a few inches wide. Again these machines can work with repositionable or lasting cements. A portion of these machines will likewise work with attractive mediums or act like laminators.

Editing devices can be as basic as a lot of scissors or paper trimmers to circle and other shape cutters. A paper trimmer will enable you to edit your photos by removing foundation areas that discourage the genuine significance of the film. Paper trimmers are likewise useful for resizing your papers to mount photos. Paper trimmers can cut straight lines, and some can likewise go with additional edges to cut scallop and wavy edges.

Each scrapbooker will have a wide assortment of pages. Card stock will be helpful. Card stock is somewhat more unwieldy, but it is incredible for making cards and mounting pictures. Card stock will come in the most basic hues, but can also be designed, finished, metallic, and sparkled. Papers also come in different loads and styles. There is vellum, lighter weight papers, mulberry, and more. Paper turns out each day in various loads and mediums. This is the thing that makes scrapbooking so energizing because the options are endless. Papers come in 12x12, 8x11, or 5x5 configurations. Collections likewise come in comparable measurements with the goal that your scrapbook pages will fit.

Embellishments incorporate stripes, eyelets, catches, stickers, brads, chipboard, and die cuts. Anything is possible with components, but a few designs require extra apparatuses. To work with eyelets, you will need an eyelet setter and a gap punch. Die cuts can be acquired, or you can utilize electronic machines like circuits or manual instruments like snappy slices to cut your die cuts. Manual and electric die cutters are for the more experienced scrapbooker.

For any individual who is an enthusiastic scrapbooker or simply appreciates making expert-looking signs and specialties, you have the Cricut Expressions.

If exactness and supreme accuracy are absolute necessities, the Cricut Expression machine might be for you.

Lately, they have released many units with various components that take into account the assorted needs of the customers. In addition to the basic machines, they've included items that can further improve the Cricut machines.

The Cricut Expression is the most widely used choice for clients. The key explanation is size. The Cricut Expression can fit increasingly vigorous tangle sizes of 12" x 24", which means it is possible to give more structures to a solitary cut. It will be simpler to make more cuts using a solitary tangle by running the machine once.

The bigger tangle size likewise encourages you to make bigger plans, room designs or even standards, for example. This is positively the best quality machine since increasingly complex structures frequently require more space, and the Cricut Expression can deal with it effortlessly.

In any case, this bigger unit also has its drawbacks. For example, it loses its transportability. Along these lines, it is intended to remain in one spot rather than having the ability to move around like the other cutting machines.

The Cricut Expression is also packaged with new presets, which will make your work simpler and help accelerate your creation. The Mix 'n Match highlight empowers you to program distinctive imaginative cuts for each character, and it will all fit into only one cutting project.

On the off chance that you wish to redo a structure design, use the AutoFill highlight - this will copy the plan to fit in however many iterations as could reasonably be expected onto a solitary piece.

Another paper saving element is the Fit to Page preset. It'll increase the size of the plan as large as conceivable to change in accordance with the majority of the page.

When you need to make cuts in bunches, the Quantity highlight will ask you what number of patterns are you needing and take you through each stacking mats.

Pictures and shapes can be flipped just by only choosing the Flip element.

Thick paper cuts are additionally not an issue, given that the Multi-Cut element will gradually shape the cutting edge. Thusly, it is precise each time it cuts.

A few cuts need an alternate beginning position. The Center Point choice will situate the cutting edge to the center of the tangle.

To have the option to keep taking a shot at a recently cut paper, you may choose the Line Return, and it will situate itself to the following line after a cut has been made.

Different highlights incorporate language determination and changing the metric estimations. There is likewise an Xtra catch which can be customized to work with components that will be released eventually.

In case you're thinking of getting yourself a Cricut Expression for work, or possibly for no reason in particular, at that point we've composed a straightforward audit that you might be keen on perusing before you get one of these machines.

1. What the hell is a Cricut?

A Cricut is a brand of cutting machine that you can use for a wide range of creating ventures. It takes plans that you make or transfer (like those you get free from us) into their Design Space programming and removes them.

It sounds straightforward, yet I ensure that you will be stunned at the number of activities you can make in a small amount of time compared to making them by hand. I'm talking sewing designs, organizer stickers, wooden signs for your home, monogrammed mugs, and much more!

This machine is ideal for the inventive individual who consistently needs to do DIY projects but lacks the time, so they sit on your Pinterest page. Also, if you have a custom made business or Etsy shop, you could get a huge amount of incentive out of this machine.

2. Would I be able to transfer my pictures to use with Cricut?

Of course! You can transfer your pictures, or any of our free SVG and Me cut records that are as of now arranged to be good with Cricut Design Space.

There are a wide range of picture document types out there. The best kind (that we give) are SVGs, which stands for (lemme put on my geeky glasses here) versatile vector realistic. It utilizes numerical recipes to make the picture focus between lines. Try not to stress – I can see your eyes staring off into the great unknown, so I won't go in more detail than that.

The advantage of this is the SVG designs can be amplified without getting that hazy, pixelated look you see with other record types, making them incredible for making tasks of any size!

3. What various materials would I be able to cut with Cricut?

Everybody will, in general, consider Cricut machines as cutting paper or vinyl, yet the fact of the matter is there are a LOT more things that a Cricut can cut. The Cricut Explore Air 2 can cut more than 60 sorts of materials!

For example, it can cut chipboard, balsa (excessively slight) wood, magnet material, aluminum (like the kind soft drinks are packaged in), and much more! For thicker materials, you will need to move up to the elevated cut sharp edge for the best cut quality.

You can also take advantage of the Cricut frequent-buyer system, which rewards clients for their buys. Brilliant organizations can issue prizes to keep clients steadfast and returning to them, over and over again. Offer your creative ventures and get great prizes that will drastically decrease your expense of vinyl for your specialty shaper!

Cricut prizes are interesting because they explicitly target cutting machine clients. We adore our art cutters and are always acquiring different kinds of products. The Cricut vinyl, for example. Vinyl has turned out to be prominent because of its usability, assortment of hues and availability of sizes and lengths. The same number of us are very cost aware; we need the best appreciation when acquiring our Cricut supplies. Reward projects help decrease the general expense of our provisions while rewarding our faithfulness to the organizations that notice our buys.

Vinyl Cricut prizes are increasingly accommodating. Since vinyl has such a significant number of employments in the art showcase, Cricut vinyl merchants are rewarding their clients with prizes based on the number and frequency of their purchases. Some vinyl Cricut providers offer partner programs that pay clients for advertising their Cricut vinyl supply sites to their friends and family. Everybody loves rewards, and what arrangement is superior to FREE vinyl for your Cricut. Sharing takes only a moment and little energy for such an extraordinary advantage.

Inventive Cricut vinyl supply organizations are offering credits to their clients who are eager to share. Credits are earned as Cricut clients transfer and show the interesting Cricut documents they have made using Cricut vinyl. This method is pretty successful in decreasing the general expense of vinyl supplies and advancing the Cricut vinyl supply organization as a trustworthy hotspot for other Cricut clients to buy their vinyl supplies. Organizations with vision are executing Cricut reward programs and will keep on making long term, win-win relations with their clients.

In summary, Cricut prizes are perhaps the most straightforward approaches to set aside loads of cash on the general expense and responsibility for the Cricut shaper or individual specialty vinyl shaper. Imaginative record sharing is fun and prizes the individuals who are eager to give others a chance at the very Cricut vinyl ventures they made. As you invest energy making mementos for yourself, you can likewise get Cricut rewards that help pay you back for your time!

There are a few die cutting machines available, including the Cuttlebug and Sizzix. These machines utilize the conventional technique for die cutting which includes setting paper over a format, covering it with a defensive board, and running it physically through a press machine to punch out the shape. This strategy is compelling and can cut numerous impressions of a picture without a moment's delay. However, there are a few confinements with regards to determination, stockpiling, and size.

The Cricut machine has reshaped the world of die cutting. It is an altogether electronic machine. The conventional dies have been replaced with little cartridges jam-packed with pictures and other alternatives. The round is like a USB thumb drive in that it has a little plug that fits into the front of the machine, stores massive amounts of information on it, is short, simple to store, and is compact. The Cricut capacities, by having the client embed the cartridge, spread the machine keypad with the custom cartridge keypad and selects the desired pictures. By using the round, the client has more alternatives. They can print products of the equivalent or various models, pick embellishments like shadows or italics, and, above all, change the size! The ability to alter the size is perhaps the best element of the Cricut machine, providing the client with the opportunity to change a picture to accommodate their structure format. The Cricut machine has size modification that can go as little as wanted, although you need to restrict this to guarantee picture quality, and it would max be able to cut out a size 12X12 or 12X24. The PC inside the machine tracks past cuts and realizes how much space is left on the rest of the paper, changing the design if there are space issues and when cutting different pictures realizes which segments have been used. This opens up a universe of possibilities that were never before possible with conventional die cutting machines.

In any case, the machine isn't perfect. The Cricut articulation, like the customary machines, can be used to cut an assortment of materials including card stock, paper, vellum, plastic, elastic, and vinyl, yet the client must make sure to alter the cutting settings or the result will be a miss-cut and harming the cutting edge of the material. The Cricut articulation requires the use of oddly shaped, tight-fitting mats which the paper should be appended to for inclusion and cutting. This implies these sheets should be obtained constantly and if the organization chooses to quit making their machine or extras, the clients will never again have the option to use the device; this isn't an issue for the customary die cutters which don't require uncommon hardware. The firmness of the cutting mat can likewise be an issue; when the floor coverings are first utilized they are exceptionally sticky and can harm the paper, making it tear or twist when released. However, after a few uses, it winds up simpler to manage. If a client finds a structure they like by another organization, for example, they are out of luck since they can't use it in the Cricut. They could use it with their Sizzix Big Shot or Cuttlebug machine which gives more opportunity in picking an organization and the pictures accessible. In the end, the gadget enables it to do die cuts where the Sizzix and Cuttlebug can do embellishing and put wrinkle marks into a paper, which offers a more extensive scope of choices for their clients.

By and large, the Cricut articulation is an amazing instrument for any paper crafter. Like all instruments, it has positives and negatives, and it is up to the end client to do the examination and choose what is right for them. The Cricut has lately become compatible with PC programming, enabling clients to plan a *format on their PC and send it to the machine to open it to the computerized and PC world of making. A comparative gadget is coming out for Sizzix, but won't require a workstation. Using a handheld gadget and electronic shaper is fundamentally the same as the Cricut. With the majority of the choices, it is a simple decision. If you need more choice in sizes, a Cricut may be for you. But if you favor flexibility, the capacity to do emblazoning, and need to utilize other brand dies, at that point a customary shaper would be the better decision.*

Scrapbooking is the most ideal approach to save your family's photographs, memorabilia, and stories. Besides, you get the opportunity to demonstrate your imaginative side by planning a Scrapbook for a specific occasion in your life.

With regards to Scrapbooking, having your energy, style, and inventiveness is an absolute necessity. There are huge amounts of books and magazines to give you ideas, however, you have to discover your own personality with regards to Scrapbooking. The magazine may have the most awesome format, but the shading plan might be one you despise. In that case, you would do better to examine it for a considerable length of time and use the hues you like. Keep in mind, assembling these recollections in an accumulation is an extension of you.

Conclusions

Cricut may seem complicated at first, but there is a lot you can do with this machine – and a lot that you can get out of it. If you feel confused by Cricut, then take your time, get familiar with the buttons, and start having fun with it.

With Cricut, anything is possible. If you've been wondering what you can do with your machine, the simple answer is almost anything. For designers, for those who like to make precise cuts, and for those who like to print their own shirts, this is a wonderful option to consider. If you are thinking of getting a Cricut machine, you'll see here that there is a lot that you can do with this unique tool, and endless creative possibilities.

The next step is simple – if you have a Cricut machine, get familiar with it. Learn more about it and see for yourself some of the fun things you can do with Cricut, and the cool basic projects you can try now.

It can help you make a lot of handmade things which not only save you money but your time as well blessing you with beautiful products that you can use for yourself as well as the gift to others. You can make handmade cards, design your t-shirt, create your ornaments, and design an envelope and many more.

If you have yet to purchase your first machine, I hope this helps your decision. We want you to enjoy Cricut projecct ideas and much as thousands of users around the world. Keep the tips and tricks provided close by as a reference guide so you aren't searching all over to find the answers to your questions.

Never stop doing research. Never stop trying new things. Never, ever stop being creative. The Cricut does not make you any less creative; it just makes the process easier so that you can focus your valuable time and efforts on more important things or personalizing the projects after making the cuts. It takes the tedious work out of your hands and makes everything fun, easy, and fast.

Nowadays everyone could use a little extra cash. Your first of many cricut projects will be to make an assortment of about 10 to 12 cards. Be creative, there are a ton of ideas you can think of. Included in this assortment you should have a couple of Birthday cards (make sure you make cards for women, men and also cards for children), make sure to include Thank You, Anniversary, Get Well and even a Sympathy card.

CRICUT PROJECTS IDEAS

An advanced guide for improving your cricut skills and become a master in your crafts. A useful guide with step-by-step methods for your creations.

Introduction

Cricut is the newest of a selection of private digital cutting machines specializing in die cutting items for home decoration, scrapbooking, paper cutting, card making, and much more. Everything you can do using a Cricut is only restricted by your creativity. These machines include Cricut cartridges for simple use. The cartridges consist of numerous amazing built-in templates for a variety of functions and dimensions.

This device is also very simple to take care of. The layouts can be selected from the cartridge or can be custom manufactured using the Cricut design studio to take your imagination to higher heights - but a computer is needed for this objective.

The Cricut package includes the following:

• Cricut machines: These are the resources which perform the real cutting because of your creative layouts.

• Gypsy: This is actually the total Cricut cartridge library at one go. It's a hand-held apparatus that features the entire Cricut design studio - so anytime we need to operate on a layout, the gypsy is conveniently available.

• Cricut Design Studio: It's the full-fledged program for creating any layout on a Cricut cutter. All you will need is a PC. One disappointment to your clients is the Cricut Design Studio isn't mac compatible. In addition, it can be used to readily Explore, cut and layout the whole cartridge library. The program also offers a choice to save the layout for future demands. Assessing a Cricut layout has never been simpler!

• Cuttlebug: It's the private die cutting and embossing system. It comprises various sizes and styles such as paper-crafting, home decoration, house jobs, events, and college projects. The plan is produced by top artists and provides sharp die cuts each and every time. Cuttlebug also includes professional excellent embossing for connections using its different feel and measurements, which makes it an amazing system.

• Cricut cake: This is an optional piece of equipment used for creating designer confectioneries for cakes and other treats, in virtually no time.

• Cricut Expression: This is an advanced version that may be used for sheets as large as 24" x 12", so it can fit any aspect, be it professional or personal. Additionally, it boasts of several cartridges and innovative options, such as the adding of colours, printing, and much more, which makes it perfect for many projects.

Cricut is the handicraft enthusiast's best friend, or for anybody who likes to design and create. It provides over 250 different designs in various sizes. The layouts could be smaller than an inch or bigger up to one inch. The 8 different cutting angles provide precision reduction - all this together with appealing templates and stylized alphabets, offers much to pick from.

Before you buy your very first Cricut, it is important to consider all probable options to decide on the very best machine to match your crafting needs.

First, you must stock up on the fundamentals, such as Cricut ribbon and picture cartridges. These cartridges come in a variety of topics to showcase and commemorate any event, like vacations or forthcoming events. You'll also need a large quantity of coloured paper, along with a pad on which to cut that contrasts to the dimensions of your system.

If you are an avid scrapbooker, you ought to start looking into buying your first Cricut cutter or the Cricut Expression. This system will cut shapes, letters and themes to decorate your scrapbook pages. It is also possible to decorate bulletin boards, posters, party decorations, greeting cards or invitations of any sort. These cutters can also cut cloth. It's encouraged for you to starch the cloth first so as to make the job as simple as possible for your own system to finish. The gap between both is straightforward.

The Cricut Expression is a brand new, 12" x 24" version of the first Cricut. This system makes it easier to create large-scale jobs in a massive quantity – as long as you've got the right quantity of paper. Font and picture cartridges may be utilised in the two machines.

Have you heard of the Cricut Cake? This useful cutter is designed to cut nearly anything for baked products, such as frosting sheets, gum paste, fondant, cookie dough, tortillas, baking soda, gum and the majority of other soft food substances. Whatever material you choose to use must be between 1/6" and 1/8" thick. Keep the blade clean at all times so as to make sure you get the very best cut possible.

Another favourite Cricut option is the Cricut Cuttlebug. This system is small. It merely cuts paper that's 6 inches wide and weighs just 7 lbs. The Cuttlebug is mainly used for cutting and embossing specific crafts. This is the best way to decorate several greeting card type invitations. Once you include a range of coloured dies, the Cuttlebug is ready to emboss straight away.

These dies are also harmonious with Sizzix, Big Shot and Thin Cuts machines, which serve a similar function.

Are you currently curious and are creating your personal t-shirts and cloth designs? Cricut also created the Yudu for all those crafters who love screen-printing and producing their own layouts. The Yudu enables its owners to attach it to a laser ink jet printer and make a layout to screen-print onto virtually anything! Yudus are used for straps, handbags, photograph frames, shoes - you name it.

Finally, if you would like to feed your newfound Cricut obsession, go right ahead and buy one of the newest Cricut Gypsys. This useful, hand-held apparatus will keep your font cartridges ready for simple portable use. It's possible to design from anyplace on the move, in the physician's office, even while on holiday, or merely sitting on your sofa. Anything you plan on the Gypsy is totally transferable to a Cricut device for die cutting. If you save your layout, it may be linked to one of your Cricut apparatus and published at a later moment.

This is a short overview of some of the cutting-edge machines Cricut sells. As you can see there's a fantastic assortment of machines for whichever specific kind of craft you wish to concentrate on. One thing is for certain. Whichever machine you select you will have many hours of inspiration and fun producing and creating your own crafting projects.

Cricut is your go-to brand for a selection of private digital cutting machines specializing in die cutting of items for home decoration, scrapbooking, paper cutting, card making, and much more. Everything you can do using a Cricut is only restricted by your creativity.

<u>Complex Cricut suggestions for the craft project</u>

Cricut private cutters are carrying handcrafts to a whole new level. People throughout the country are astonished at the amazing and advanced Cricut thoughts this machine may bring to your job listing. You can create almost anything amazing and one of a kind working with the Cricut cartridges.

How does a Cricut machine function? It is very straightforward. Simply load a Cricut cartridge to the machine, choose what colour card stock you would like to use for your individual layout and cut off. Each cartridge has different themed layouts from seasonal layouts to favourite cartoon characters. You can pick from the cut-out layouts to use for scrapbooks, picture frames, customized greeting cards, wall hangings, calendars and a lot more.

One of the amazing Cricut ideas it is possible to create as a craft is the Cricut calendar. Every month can be produced in another page and you'll be able to decorate these pages using various layouts. Wouldn't it be wonderful to make your February page employing the Love-struck Season cartridge? The Easter cartridge will supply you with endless layouts for the April page of the calendar. Your May calendar could be made with the Mother's Day cartridge.

How interesting would it be to style your July page with trimmings made with the Independence Day season cartridge? December can be outfitted together with All the Joys of the Season cartridge and the Snow Friend's cartridge. You may select items to your heart's content.

Another fantastic idea you may make is a scrapbook. This well-loved craft job is why Cricut cutting machine were devised in the first place. Together with the Cricut die cutting machine, you can personalize scrapbooks for your kids, for mother-daughter or dad and son keepsakes. Cricut created cartridges that each little child would delight in using like the Once Upon a Princess cartridge or the Disney Tinker Bell and Friends' cartridge. Your small superhero would certainly love the Batman layout in the Batman: The Brave and the Bold or Robots cartridges. Cricut provides you lots of layouts to select from for scrapbooking ideas.

The Cricut layouts aren't only layout ideas, but additionally have fonts and alphabets in the Sesame Street font cartridge along with the Ashlyn's alphabet cartridge. Use these exciting tools when making your personalized gift like a wall-hanging picture frame for framing a photograph of an unforgettable occasion of the receiver of your gift. Embellish your wall hanging with pretty cut-outs produced by the Cricut cutter.

Your Cricut ideas are endless by means of this superb machine and also the Cricut cartridges to suit any event and job possible to consider. Creating a Cricut job with the entire family is a superb way to spend some time together and producing those gorgeous items can be a superb experience for everyone to achieve.

Ideas that could generate income

People really feel the Cricut machine is the one instrument that's responsible for the conceptualization of those layouts which we see in scrapbooks. In fact, the designs are derived in the brain of the consumer and are made concrete by the Cricut cutting machine.

In addition, there are other tools which help create the layouts such as cartridges and applications tools. The top software tool out there's is the Cricut Design Studio. With this application, you can create and edit your own designs and also edit current designs which are pre-packed.

Life is great indeed! People also believe the use of a Cricut cutting system is only restricted to the area of scrapbooking. Only a few men and women may know, but the Cricut machine in addition to the cartridges and the software tools may be used for a large number of things. There are a whole lot of Cricut projects which it is possible to use the Cricut cutting system for and only your mind can restrict what you could do.

Greeting cards are excellent Cricut projects for everyone to participate in. Together with the layouts you may receive from the Cricut cartridge along with the software tools you have set up; you can lay out covers that withstand the unconventional. The difficulty most men and women experience when they attempt to buy greeting cards is they can't find the type of card they're searching for. This may result in stress and a great deal of frustration on the purchaser's part. You're so much better off making your own personal greeting cards.

Cricut calendars are another fantastic reason to get a Cricut cutting device. A calendar is full of 12 months. You can get creative and search for layouts on your cartridge or software which could reflect the month that's inside your calendar. If we're at the month of December, then you can search for layouts that fit the mood and feeling of December. Start looking for snowmen, reindeers, and Christmas trees. I promise you that you have all of the layouts you will ever desire inside of your own software or cartridge.

Keep in mind, only your imagination can restrict what you do. These Cricut projects may be used either for individual satisfaction or revenue generating functions. Be imaginative with your Cricut machine. You never know what crazy thoughts can pop into your mind.

From the universe of record making, an individual may believe there are only hardware resources such as the Cricut cutting machine, as well as the Cricut Expression system. But there also are software tools which may help you create great Cricut ideas that could help you in the creation of your perfect scrapbook.

One of them is your Cricut Design Studio. This software tool is a fresh method for connecting your initial machine to your own computer and it may also works with the Cricut Expression. With the usage of an onscreen cutting mat, this program tool allows Explore, layout, and cutting from the whole Cricut cartridge library. The excellent thing about this is what you see is what you cut! Additionally, this application has an interface which is extremely user - friendly and has the capacity to store any of your own creations. This is a tool which any scrapbooker should get!

With this tool, it is possible to do anything and create countless Cricut ideas. The general rule here is to allow your creativity to know no limitations. When you make a scrapbook, the most important objective is to make layouts that jive with all the images you set in. Let us say for instance, you add some pictures of your wedding day.

You need to select or create a layout that will make an impression that could make anybody who looks at the images and the scrapbooks relive the memories. The exact same general rule will apply to anybody. You might even generate income out of this by helping people develop designs for their scrapbook.

The usage of the computer software isn't confined to only creating scrapbooks. As stated, earlier, let your creativity set the limitations and there should be no limitations. Besides scrapbooks, the next things you can make include: a. Wall hangings b. Image frames c. Greeting cards

Maybe the most frequent innovation of the Cricut machine aside from scrapbooks is Cricut calendars. The layouts which you receive from a Cricut system may be used to include spice and life to any calendar. With the usage of a Cricut machine in addition to the software applications, you may produce layouts for every month in a calendar year. The trick is to pick any layout that could reflect exactly what that particular month is all about. October for instance where the very best layout is always a backdrop depicting Oktoberfest.

So, there you've got it, a few excellent Cricut ideas which could help you make money or just simply make you happier. Bear in mind, it's your own choice. Get ready to have a rocking good time!

A broad variety of cartridges can be found on the market, although not all these cartridges operate with all sorts of machines. As an example, the Cricut cartridge operates with Cricut machines only, and it's the vital element whereby crafters and artists can create many designs in wonderful colours and styles.

Together with the changes in printing technologies, a selection of cartridges was introduced recently with more packages to pick from compared to prior ones. The two main kinds of printer cartridges available are: the ink (used with an ink-jet printer), and laser cartridges, used in laser printers. In the case of all Cricut machines, they still use ink-jet printers easily.

All about Cricut ink cartridges:

At first, Cricut ink cartridges were only available in black, but after some time, a few different colours were introduced. Afterwards, together with advancements in printing technology, ink cartridges have been developed, and attempts were made to present different font styles, layout and colours for forming contours, too.

The key to the success of the Cricut system, is the use of distinct and special kinds of cartridges that enable users to obtain, cut and create in almost any font, layout, colour and design.

The general types of Cricut cartridges are:

- Font cartridge: It includes full alphabets, numbers and other symbols together with font styles and other font organizing shapes. Some of the favourite all-year seasonal and around cartridges comprise Forever Young, Jasmine, Teardrop, Lyrical Letters, Pumpkin carving for Halloween, Thanksgiving holiday, Winter Wonderland for the Christmas season, etc.

- Shape cartridge: It includes an assortment of shapes including boxes, tags, bags, animals, sports, paper dolls, etc.

- Licensed cartridge: It enables users to find the cut designed with favourite figures such as Disney's Micky Mouse, Hello Kitty, Pixar's Toy Story, etc.

- Classmate cartridge: As its name implies, is made specifically for classroom functions, which includes classroom fonts, shapes and classroom layout, visual analysis program, suggestions and representations of educators, etc.

- Solutions cartridge: It costs less than the rest. The shapes include welding, baseball, soccer, campout, etc.

The wide variety of Cricut cartridges, as mentioned above, provides crafters, particularly young customers, an opportunity to experiment with their artistic skills without the support of a computer, whereas the Cricut ink cartridge makes it a lot easier for them to create designs in a variety of shapes and colours.

Projects Design (Starting A New Project, Machine Reset, Basic Objects Editing)

One unique feature of the Cricut Design space is the ability to personalize your projects using text, images and distinct font styles. This is one unique feature I am super excited about. What makes Design Space unique is that you get the freedom to express your creative mind in so many ways.

If you are already familiar with design space, you might find it easy to customize designs and work with the exciting features therein. However, if you are beginner, you'll need a basic walk through to get you well acquainted with the basic design operations.

So to start off, I like to take you through the steps you can use to add text, select font, install/uninstall font in Windows/Mac and how to use images in Design Space.

How to Add Text in Cricut Design Space

1. Select the Text tool located at the left-hand side of the Canvas for computer users and for iOS or Android App user, you can find the Text tool at the bottom-left of your screen.

2. Choose your desired font type and size and then type in your text. Use the 'Return' key to start a new line of text on the same textbox. Do not freak out when you discover that you did not select the font settings before inputting your text. This is because it is possible, with Design Space, for you to type in the text before selecting the font settings on a Windows/Mac computer.

3. Click or tap, depending on your device, on any area outside the textbox to close it.

How to Edit Text in Cricut Design Space

Of course, your first task is to add the text to your Canvas. After that you can begin to edit the text to suite your design. There are a number of things you can do with the Edit tool including the size, font and even rotate the text. Here is a simple step by step approach to editing the text on the Canvas.

Editing the text is super simple. Double click on the text to display the available options. Select your desired action from the list of options displayed. You can tinker with the font style, the font type, font size, letter spacing and line spacing. These options can be accessed in the Edit bar.

For Windows or Mac users, the Edit bar is located at the top of the Canvas while for iOS or Android users, the Edit bar is found at the bottom of the Canvas. Now, you can play around with the

Edit tool to get conversant with it. This tool is very important for working with Cricut machines and most especially Design Space. Below is what the tools look like:

How to Write Using Fonts

The instructions are different depending on your platform. The instructions for Windows/Mac, iOS and Android are given below:

For Windows/Mac

1. Select 'Text' in the design panel located at the left-hand side of the canvas.

2. From the Text Edit bar that will appear, input the text or you can even select the font before the inputting the text.

3. Click the Font drop-down menu to select the "System" index which will display only the font installed on the computer.

4. Select the font you desire.

For Android:

1. Navigate to the bottom of the screen and select 'Text'.

2. From the displayed font list, search or scroll through the list to find your desired System font from the available fonts. Note that System fonts will be labeled 'System'.

3. Select the font you desired and then type in your text.

<u>For iOS:</u>

1. Go to the bottom of the Canvass screen and select 'Text'.

2. Select the "System" index from the font list that appears to display only the installed fonts on your device.

3. Select the font you desire and type in your text.

<u>How to Edit Fonts</u>

The Edit bar in Cricut Design Space grants you access to alter the features of images or text. These features include Linetype, Size, Fill, Rotate, Position, mirror and so on. So how do we edit the font? It is super easy! Just follow the steps below:

1. Select your desired text object to be edited on the Canvas. Alternatively, you can select a text layer from the Layers Panel or insert the text from the design panel. Once the text has been selected, the Text Edit Bar will pop up directly below the Standard Edit Bar.

2. When the Text Edit Bar pops up, you can now begin to manipulate the font with the options described below.

Font - like its name, this option will display both the Cricut fonts and System fonts saved in your computer. I will discuss system fonts shorty.

Font filter - this option allows you to choose, your preference by category, which fonts will appear in the Font Type menu. There are a number of font filters which are described below:

- All Fonts- this displays the available fonts (Cricut fonts and System fonts)
- System Fonts- this display the fonts found on your computer
- Cricut Fonts- this displays font from the Cricut Library
- Single-Layer Fonts- this display fonts containing just one layer
- Writing Style Fonts- these display fonts that are specifically designed written by pen.

Style - this option allows you to select the font style including italic, bold, regular, bold italic and writing style. It is important to note that the style options for Cricut fonts are different from that of System fonts.

Font Size - this option allows you to change the size of the font using the point size. You can either type the point size value or use steppers to increase the value in steps of one (1).

Letter Space - this allows you to change the space between letters. As noted in Font size, you can type in the value or use the steppers.

Line Space - this enables you to alter the spacing between rows of text.

Alignment - this allows you to position the entire block of text to the left, right or center or even have full justification.

Curve - this enables you to bend the text into circular shape. For a crafter, this is a good option when you want to design write-ups for curved materials such as tumblers, bowls and buckets.

Advanced - this allows you to create individual groupings of text, letters, lines and layers of text. There are three sub-options under this option as described below

- Ungroup to Letters- this is used to ungroup letters in the text box into separate layers. With this option, each letter will be seen as a separate layer and will show up as image in the Layers Panel. You can now edit the letters independently while keeping each layer grouped together.

- Ungroup to Lines- this is used to ungroup rows of text in the text box into separate layers with each line viewed as a separate layer. Each line will now show up as a separate image in the Layer's Panel. You can also edit the lines independently while keeping each layer grouped together.

- Ungroup to Layers- this is used to ungroup multilayered text to allow each group of layers to appear as an image in the Layers Panel. The text will appear as an image and the letters will still be grouped together. Therefore, you can edit the layers independently.

System Fonts

System fonts refer to fonts installed on your computer or mobile device. Every time you sign in, the Cricut Design Space will automatically access your system fonts and allow you to use them for free in the Design Space projects.

It is important to state here that some system fonts are not compatible with Cricut Design space because they were not designed by Cricut. Therefore, do not be surprise when you encounter failure when trying to import them into the Design Space or behave in an unusual manner when using them in the Design Space.

Cutting Instructions for Materials

This is more like tips and tricks for cutting materials and you may want to know why these cutting instructions are important? The reason is simply for precision. As you are probably aware, the Cricut machine was designed to cut materials with precision and accuracy. But to do these require some set of instructions that will make that possible.

So, ensure that you follow the steps below to avoid frustrations in terms of money, materials and wasted time. These are very simple steps and made easy for your understanding.

1. Start by placing the material on the mat

2. Ensure that all the four edges of the material are taped to the mat. It is recommended that it should be at least 1' from each of the corners.

3. Move the White Star Wheels on the Cricut machine to the right. This will ensure that no imprint is left on the material by the Star Wheel.

4. Clean the front metal bar if you desire to cut thicker material. Again, make sure that no part of the material is allowed to move under the rubber rollers in order to avoid jamming of the Cricut machine.

5. Do a test a cut to ensure that the edges are properly cut before cutting the main material. The essence of this is to correct probable errors that might arise such as a blunt blade.

You definitely know that thicker materials will take more time to cut than thinner materials. This is due to the fact that thicker materials will require multiple cut-passes and also the fact that the cut pressure increases gradually while cutting thick materials.

Cutting Instructions for Cricut Craft Foam

1. Place the material, in this case Craft Foam, unto the Cricut Strong Grip Mat and make sure the grain is aligned vertically.

2. Select the size and image.

3. Load the mat into Cricut machine.

4. Select Browse All Materials.

5. From the list of materials, select Craft Foam.

6. Press the Go button.

It is recommended that you avoid cutting intricate images less than 2" x 2". This is more like a standard procedure and maybe to avoid error while cutting.

How to Use Images in Cricut Design Space

There are more than 50,000 images in the Cricut Library. With the Design space, you have permission to try these images for free in order to confirm its suitability in your desired project or projects and then after that you can purchase it.

You can also upload personal images unto the Canvas.

So, how do you use images in Cricut Design Space? Here are simple steps on how to use images in your project:

1. Create a new project by signing in to your Design Space

2. Click on Images located at the left-hand side of the design screen if you are using Windows/Mac computer or tap on Image button situated at the bottom left corner of the design screen if you are using iOS/Android device.

You can also browse, filter and search the images in order to choose the ones you intend to use in your project:

I.   All Images - use this option to search for a particular image in your Cricut Library or even view featured images

II.   Categories - use this option is more like filter tool. It is used to browse images by selecting any one of the image categories.

III.   Cartridges - use this option to search through the list of 400+ Cricut cartridges alphabetically or even search for a specific one.

3. Insert the desired image(s) into your project

4. Edit the images as much as you like.

<u>How to Print Then Cut Using Your Cricut Machine</u>

I will begin by getting an image/project unto your Cricut Design Space, print it out with your Printer (usually inkjet) and then cut the design with your Cricut machine in a step by step fashion.

The first thing to do when you want to achieve this is to first start with your Cricut Design Space. So, let's go there:

Step One: Cricut Design Space

First of all, you know that you can access the Cricut Design Space using your regular internet devices. Right? Good. It doesn't matter the Operating System used by that device because a lot of these devices are compatible with the Cricut Design Space program.

It is widely known that majority of our regular internet devices use either Windows OS, Mac OS, Android OS or iOS. You don't have any problem what OS that you have on your device as we will discuss how to upload or place an image unto the Canvas of the Cricut Design Space using each of these OS. By this, no one is left behind.

First, let us start with the Windows/Mac OS on a laptop/notebook.

On Windows/Mac

The first thing to do is to open your Cricut Design Space which will show the canvas area as displayed below

1. Choose Upload on the design panel which you can located at the bottom left of the Canvas.

You can drag and drop the file you intend to use unto the upload window or you can select browse to locate your desired file from your compute.

2. Remember that you can upload Basic Image or Vector Image. For now, we will not bother ourselves with the technicalities of these images. What we want to achieve is to get an image unto the canvas using the options below:

• Select and then open your desired image file or you can drag and drop the file unto the canvas. As you know, there are over 50,000 images you can play with in the Cricut Design Space library and the number will increase with your own customized images on your computer.

• From the screen, choose what best describes your desired image type. It can be simple, moderately complex or complex

• Click Continue

• Do you have unwanted background in the image you intend to edit? If so, then you need to define the cut lines of your image using Select & Erase. You can also use Erase and Crop. When you have removed the unwanted background, move to the next option.

• Select the Preview to view the cut lines of your image. The essence of this option is to find out if you are okay with the image you want to print and if you are not satisfied with the preview, you can hide the preview to edit your image again.

• If you are satisfied with the image, select Continue.

• Give your image a name and tag it.

• Select Save. To ensure that your image save properly, click on Print and Cut before clicking on Save button because if you click on only Cut, your image will not save properly and you may have to upload it all over again. Am sure you don't want that to happen.

   3.   After saving, the image will be uploaded into your uploaded images.

4. Select the image and insert it into the Canvas.

5. Resize it to suit your desired project.

6. Click Make It. Your image will be shown with a black bounded box.

7. Select Continue.

So, you have finished your first step with the Cricut Design Space and you now ready to print. Jump to the Print Section to continue the steps.

Materials You Can Use In The Machine

Most people believe that they can only cut paper and vinyl with the Cricut machine. You will soon find once you get started using your machine that it can actually cut different types of materials! Material finishes ranging from fun and flashy, to polished and rich. These materials make it easy to achieve exactly the look you are after. Once you get more comfortable using all the different types of materials, you will easily be able to create projects that have multiple materials in one! The more you know, the better your project will be!

Vinyl

Adhesive vinyl for Cricut cutting machines come in a wide variety of colors, designs, and uses. The adhesive properties

can either be semi-permanent (easily removable with adhesive remover) or permanent. Semi-permanent is typically used for projects indoors; such as wall decals or window clings. Permanent vinyl would be used for outdoor use, such as holiday décor and tabletop designs. Those are perfect for making stickers and indoor and outdoor items, and even "printing" on mugs and T-shirts! Once you get into it, it's truly addictive to acquire different colors and types. For example, you can get chalkboard vinyl, which is awesome for labeling, or outdoor vinyl, which will look great on your car window. These materials can be purchased at virtually any craft shop, and they aren't too expensive if you do a little canvassing. Double check that it is indeed the type of vinyl you are looking for, though.

Vinyl is the most commonly used material for Cricut projects outside of paper because it is one of the most versatile materials to work with. Adhesive vinyl is a great starting point for creators who are new to Cricut but want to branch out outside of paper crafting. Adhesive vinyl is a material that will need to be weeded, as designs are typically cut out of the vinyl and the negative space will need to be removed in order to see the design.

Paper

There is a wide variety of paper products that can be cut using

the Cricut machine. Some varieties include cardstock, which is one of the most popular, corrugated cardboard, foil embossed, Kraft board, scrapbooking paper, pearl, sparkle/shimmer, and poster board. Paper products can come in a wide range of sizes, with 12"x12" being the most common and easily applied type as it fits perfectly on a 12"x12" cutting mat. Paper is most commonly used in card projects, but it can also assist in wall décor, gift boxes, cake toppers, lantern projects. Most crafters familiar with the Cricut recommend starting with the paper project first, to get a handle of the different options Cricut cutters to have. Paper allows you to create intricate designs and get familiar with cutting blade depth at the same time. What you have to remember is that you need something to practice on, and a cheap printer paper works wonderfully for that. You won't feel bad for making mistakes because the material does not cost much. If you are feeling more creative than usual, you may get the colored paper too. This way, when you get the hang of cutting, you can create letters for cars or stencils.

The following materials can only be used with the Cricut Maker machine.

Chipboard

The Cricut website sells a variety pack of this type of material, which is great for getting to know the material and what

projects to use it effectively. It is suggested for use on projects such as sturdy wall art, school projects, photo frames and more. Since this material has a 1.5mm thickness, it can only be cut using the Cricut Knife blade. Chipboard is great for any time of project that requires dimensions such as gingerbread or haunted house around the holidays!

Fabric

The fabric is great if you have the Cricut Maker. Chances are that you will want to cut some textile with this machine on hand; that's why you should stock up on that and get extra just in case. You can obtain some cheap, scrappy fabrics to practice on before moving on to the proper fabrics for the projects.

This simple yet classic material is another favorite among Cricut Maker users. Many use fabrics to create custom clothing, home décor, and wall art. Imagine all the times you went out looking for the perfect top or skirt only to come back home empty handed after many hours of searching. It would be ideal to find exactly what you want when you want it! Now, without the help of a bulky and outdated sewing machine, you can make simple and affordable clothing exactly the look and feel you want! Fabric is also a great material to make homemade gifts for friends and family. Lots of people enjoy curling up on the couch during the winter months with a cozy

quilt and a favorite movie.

Felt

Blended fibers between natural and synthetic are also common among craft felts. Felt is commonly used to help young children distinguish among different types of textiles. Felt is also commonly used in craft projects for all ages. The felt is easily cut with your Cricut Machine, no Deep Cut blade required! Felt can be used for fun décor, kid's crafts, baby toys, stuffed shapes and more! When starting out on the Cricut Maker, this is one of the best materials to start out with. This material is very forgiving and will allow you to keep the gift- giving spirit going! This material is also great for creating faux flowers. You can bring the outside in, without the maintenance or worrying about children or pets getting into a mess!

Cardstock

If you plan on making cards or labels, cardstock is a must. The more, the better. It's really awesome to have a large pile of it and just be able to cut to your heart's content. It will also help practicing on once you have perfected cutting normal printing paper.

Fondant

Fondant is for those bakers out there. There is a possibility that you already have extra fondant lazing about in your home. However, it never hurts to have more. The awesome thing about fondant is that you can reuse it to an extent, depending on how well it freezes or how big the need is to freeze it before cutting. Of course, it is useful to have back up materials for the days that you are in a crafty sort of mood. Most materials are available on the Cricut website so you can order them along with your Cricut machine. Everything will be delivered at once, and you won't have to buy anything again for a while.

It also depends on what sort of material you will be interested in creating something awesome with. If you are going to cut wood, for instance, you will have to stock up on that as you will be going through it quite fast if you are an enthusiastic and excitable crafter.

TOOLS AND ACCESSORIES OF CRICUT

Cricut has much to offer in the way of tools and accessories. There are machines they offer to suit different crafting purposes, which have their own accessories and tools as well.

For the Cricut cutting machines, here is what's available:

Cricut Maker Cutting Blades

In addition to the Explore Cutting blade, the Cricut Maker has additional cutting blades that allow for intricate cutting details on a variety of materials.

The Cricut Maker comes with one additional blade, the revolutionary rotary cutting blade for use on cutting all sorts of fabrics. Unlike the average rotary blade, this one lasts far longer because it avoids the nicks that typically come with its line of duty. You can buy additional blades individually, but one blade should last throughout multiple projects.

Cutting Mats

Cricut cutting mats come in a variety of sizes and degree of stickiness. Depending on what material you are using, you will

want less or more stickiness on your mat, to hold the material in place while cutting.

The Circuit Weeder

The weeder tool, which looks similar to a dental pick, is used for removing negative space from a vinyl project. This weeder tool is a must when doing any type of project that involves vinyl. Trying to get rid of access vinyl is nearly impossible without a weeder especially with materials like glitter iron-on. A weeder is a useful tool for any type of project using adhesives. Instead of picking up the adhesive with your fingertips, user the weeder tool and keep your fingers sticky mess free!

The Cricut Scraper

The Circuit Scraper tool is essential (and a lifesaver!) when you need to rid your cutting mat of excess negative bits. This tool typically works best with paper, such as cardstock, but other materials can easily be scraped up as well. Use the flexibility of the mat to your advantage as you scrap the bits off the mat, to ensure you are not scraping up the adhesive on the mat as well. You can also use the Cricut Scraper as a score line holder, which allows you to fold over the score-line with a nice crisp edge. It can also be used as a burnishing tool for Cricut

transfer tape, as it will allow seamless separation of the transfer tape from the backing.

The Cricut Spatula

A spatula is a must-have tool for a crafter who works with a lot of paper. Pulling the paper off of a Cricut cut mat can result in a lot of tearing and paper curling if you are not diligent and mindful when you are removing it. The spatula is thinly designed to slip right under paper which allows you to ease it off the mat carefully. Be sure to clean it often as it is likely to get the adhesive build up on it after multiple uses. It can also be used as a scraper if your scraper tool is not readily available!

Scissors

These sharp tools come in handy more often than you can possibly know with Cricut projects and having a dedicated pair makes it so much easier to complete your projects.

Craft Tweezers

These reverse-action tweezers have a strong grip, precise points, and alleviate cramping after prolonged use.

Spatula

Sometimes you feel like you need an extra set of hands when you're peeling or laying down a project. This tool gives you that extra support and maneuverability where you need it.

Scoring Stylus

This tool can be loaded into clamp A in your Cricut machine. This will allow the machine to draw deep lines into your project to give it texture or a precise folding point. This same effect can be achieved with other tools on the market, but Cricut makes it simpler and faster with this accessory.

Portable Trimmer

This is a precision cutting tool that allows you to get fast, crisp, straight cuts on your projects 100% of the time.

Rotary Cutting Kit

This kit includes a gridded cutting mat and a rotary cutting tool. Cuts are fast, sharp, and precise. This is far from the only rotary tool available on the market, and it's great for cutting fabric and scrapbook pieces.

XL Scraper/Burnishing Tool

This provides a level of control that cannot be beaten. It exerts pressure evenly and helps to eliminate uneven layering and air bubbles. This tool comes very highly recommended by the community of users.

Paper Crafting Set – If you're particularly into papercraft, you will find the edge distresser, quilling tool, piercing tool, and craft mat in this set to be quite to your liking. Quilling or paper filigree art is gaining popularity these days and these are some of the best tools available for that craft.

TrueControl™ Knife

This is a precision blade that is comparable to XACTO in quality and in type. For more precise freehand cuts, this knife is very helpful at any crafting station.

Cricut Explore® Wireless Bluetooth® Adapter

This product is to help your Cricut Explore machine connect with Bluetooth to your computer or device. The Cricut Maker has this capability built-in, but it can be added to your Explore machine as well.

Deep-Point Replacement Blades

These help your Cricut machine to make more precise cuts with thicker materials!

Bonded Fabric Blades

These blades are meant to retain their extremely sharp point, cut after cut into fabric in your machine!

Replacement Blades

With different purposes like debossing, engraving, perforation and more, can be purchased from Cricut as well. These are specifically for the Cricut Maker model, whereas the replacement blades specified above are for the Cricut Explore models.

The Cricut Easy press

If you begin to venture into iron-on projects and want to upgrade from a traditional iron and ironing board, the Cricut Easy press is the right way to go. It will make projects so much easier than using a traditional iron. The Cricut Easy press is known to help keep designed adhered for longer, essentially no more peeling of designs after one or two uses and washes. The Easy press also takes all of the guesswork out of the right amount of contact time as well as temperature. You will not run the risk of burning your transfer paper or fabric!

The Cricut Brightpad

The lightweight and low profile design of the Cricut Brightpad

reduces eyestrain while making crafting easier. It is designed to illuminate fine lines for tracing, cut lines for weeding and so much more! It is thin and lightweight which allows for durable transportation. BrightPad makes crafting more enjoyable with its adjustable, evenly lit surface. The bright LED lights can be adjusted depending on the workspace. The only downfall to this accessory is that it must be plugged in while it is used. It does not contain a rechargeable battery.

The Cricut Cuttlebug Machine

The Cricut Cuttlebug is embossing and dies cutting machine that offers portability and versatility when it comes to cutting and embossing a wide variety of materials. This machine gives professional looking results with clean, crisp, and deep embosses. This machine goes beyond paper, allowing you to emboss tissue paper, foils, thin leather, and more!

Where To Find Materials

Cricut Machines and Cartridges can get a little pricey if you don't shop around. If the price is holding you back, then rest assured we can help you to find some great discounts and sales.

The Cricut Expression machine and the original are both a dream come true for scrapbook enthusiasts and paper craft lovers. You can make, print, and die cut almost any shape you can think of simply and easily. Just push a button and watch it work, no computer required. Scrapbook designs, custom greeting cards, party decorations, and more are made simple, easy, and quick with Provo Craft's new machine. With over 55 Cricut Cartridges to choose from, there's no shortage of project ideas you could invent.

The one downside to these machines is the price tag. They save you both time and money, but to start out they carry a hefty price of $299 for the Personal Cricut Cutting Machine and around $499 for the larger Expression machine. This is a hit on anybody's pocketbook.

Cartridges too are very expensive. These contain the shapes, fonts, and different designs that you can make your machine print. However, each add-on cartridge usually costs around $50 all the way up to $100. Add that onto the original price tag of your Cricut and you've got a huge investment! Sure you could make money with your scrapbooking, it can even pay for itself in time and money saved, and most owners swear that it is worth every dollar spent, but the initial payment is just too high for many.

The easiest way to find discount sales on cheap Cricut products is to shop around. Shop the sales at your local craft stores like Micheal's and JoAnn Fabrics. If there aren't any sales coming soon, then you can always look online. We are big fans of buying our products off of eBay since you can get some great discounts. Many times the auctions are for whole packages of cartridges and a machine. Sometimes they even throw in free bonus accessories to sweeten the deal. You can find both new and used machines for far below the sticker price.

Cheap Cricut Machines - It Is All About Amazon

Scrapbooking was not an easy process back when it was still in its infant years. The actual process was so tedious and meticulous that one small mistake was enough to make you go crazy because you had to start all over again. But with the advent in technology, things have become so much easier and more convenient. Now, we have the Cricut machine which is largely responsible for making scrapbooking so much easier than it was 50 years ago.

For those that are a bit curious about what this device is, the Cricut equipment is a home die cutting tool. It is capable of giving patterns to paper, fabric, and vinyl sheets. The designs are stored on cartridges which can be accessed via a computer that has a USB. Now isn't that cool? So if you are seriously thinking of getting into the habit of scrapbook making, the Cricut machine is a tool that you definitely must have. But remember, this can be a costly investment. However, if you know where to look then you can get cheap Cricut machines.

New Cricut equipment can cost you over $300. For the financially capable, this is no biggie. But if you are working on minimum wage and have kids to send to school and rent to pay, this can be a significant investment. The best place to look for cheap Cricut machines is on Amazon. Amazon is a site where online sellers meet and sell their goods.

The great thing about Amazon is that you get the merchandise straight from the seller and not through some channel of distribution. That's one reason why many products being sold on Amazon are significantly cheaper than what you see in the shops or boutiques at malls. Exercise precaution as there might be online sellers that are hacked. One great way to check the profile of the seller is to get their feedback rating. A feedback rating is the rating given by people whom the seller has done business with. Always aim for the 99.9 to 100% feedback rating or score.

On Amazon, you will find a combination of new and used cheap Cricut machines. Always remember, new is not always good. There might higher models of Cricut equipment that is not that old but is sold at the same price as a lower end model that is new. Go for the former. As a scrapbook maker, it is always understandable that you want the best quality tool. But you also need to be wise and practical. Enough has been said.

Ideas for Using Your Cricut

Create your own Handmade Greeting Cards

Have you ever gone into a store to buy a greeting card? It doesn't matter which type of card it is, birthday, Christmas, Easter or just friendly thinking of you card to send off to a long lost friend, you find yourself flipping it over to see the price. Usually, the price for just one greeting card is over $4.00. That is very expensive for a simple card.

Why not instead make your own handmade greeting cards with your Cricut machine and save yourself the money while creating your own personal designs? There are many different cartridges for many different fun designs. Get creative, colorful and inspired while making these cards.

Create your own seasonal decorations

Any season or holiday it is easy to come up with some of your own holiday decorations using nothing more than Cricut machines and scrapbooking supplies. Just imagine the Christmas trees, Valentine hearts or Halloween ghosts you can make.

Create your own wall lettering

Why spend hours yourself or worse yet hiring a muralist for hand-painting your favorite letters on your walls. You can easily do it yourself with vinyl die cuts which will produce almost the same look like a professional.

Make your own Die Cut stickers

Die cut stickers are a great gift for young children who just love to stick them everywhere. You can use them to create fun and colorful posters, school projects or to put in sticker books. These stickers can be made in any shape imaginable and are not as expensive as going out and buying them in a craft store.

Creative Scrapbooking Ideas

Have a child or expecting one soon? Why not create a scrapbook filled with their life! You can start with the day of their birth and keep adding photos as they grow older. When your child gets older, it will be the perfect gift (the story of their life).

Party or wedding favors

Use with the tags, boxes, bags and more cartridge to make party favor creations easy. You can make anything from hats, gifts, bags, banners or other creations tailored to your exact party or wedding theme and color.

These are some ideas that you can use to create fun projects with your Cricut machine. Explore the internet to find even more ideas. Let your imagination go wild.

Cricut Projects Ideas To Try

Let's face it! Most of us don't have the graphic design or drawing skills required to come up with jaw-dropping projects or images, but this doesn't mean you can't use the Cricut machine. On the contrary, you can find in Design Space Ready-to-Make Projects, that are created by professionals. As it turns out, these projects cover every category from fashion to paper crafting and home decor. On top of that, you can even find a few free projects. You will be able to find in this view new projects regularly.

Are you out of ideas, and you don't have enough creativity to create your own design, image, or project? Don't worry! Just find a project you like, grab your supplies, and go for it. If you want to view all Ready-to-Make projects, you will need to access the Projects page of Cricut Design Space and scroll down to see as many projects as you want. There are a few hundreds of them, but the list is refreshed with new projects quite often (so you better keep an eye on it).

If you are using a desktop computer, or a laptop you can select a Project Category from the drop-down menu located on the upper side of the screen, or if you know what you want, you can type what you need in the search bar.

The view is a bit different if you are using the Mobile App of Design Space. From the Home view, you will see the Categories drop-down, you can tap on it to see different categories, or the Search bar to find what you need.

Have you ever wondered what happens if you click on a Ready-to-Make project? Let's say that you want to use a specific project, which comes included with the Cricut Access subscription. If you click (or tap) on it, the Project Preview window will show up, where you will see all the details you need for the project, information like:

- Project Name

- Difficulty Level

- Estimated Completion Time

- Materials Required

- Instructions

When you want to use a project which is not included with your subscription plan, you will have the cost of the project as well. It's just like a recipe for a meal you want to cook.

Then, you can only have two options in Design Space:

1. "Make It" - if you want to leave the project as it is, and go straight to the mat preview screen;

2. "Customize" - if you want to add a personal touch to your project, as this option will take you to the design screen. You can "play" with the image size (or color), adjust it as you like, or add an extra image, then "Save" the project in your account. When you are finished customizing the project, click "Make It."

How to Make Your Own Projects

You will be able to open the projects in your Canvas view, or you can create a brand new one from scratch (by clicking on the New button from the Home screen). This is where you can play with the available options, as you can go to images and search for the image you want to use for your project. You will see the image opening in the Canvas view, and then you will have above the Edit Bar. You will get to Undo or Redo, your changes, Edit, Arrange, Flip, or Rotate the object you opened in this view.

If you want to add text to it, click the Text icon, and you will see the Text Bar appearing below the Edit Bar. There you can play with the options. At any point in the editing process, you will be able to see the Make It button on the top right corner of the screen. When you are finished, click it and prepare your machine for the cut: turn it on, load the mat and place the material on it. To save material, you can consolidate color on your images, as fewer colors mean fewer materials.

Practical Examples of Projects

The Cricut world is full of project ideas you can try on your Cricut machine, and the Cricut Community looks like an endless inspiration page for all the Cricut enthusiasts out there. A very popular process you can try with your Cricut machine is the HTV (Heat Transfer Vinyl). In other words, you can create your very own custom T-shirts or the most adorable baby bodysuits. Why buy custom T-shirts when you can create your own? What you need for this project:

-       A Cricut machine (from the Explore Family, or the Cricut Maker itself)

-       The Cricut Iron-On Vinyl (as material)

-       A simple T-shirt or baby bodysuit

-       A Grip Mat (Green, or Light Blue)

-       A Weeding tool

-       A Teflon Iron

- Piece of fabric of 9" x 9," to act as a buffer between the iron and the fabric

- Files from the Cricut Access subscription plan

Another very practical project idea is a paper flower decoration in a shadow box. For this project, you will need the Cricut Maker, the StandardGrip Mat, glue, tweezers, buttons, straight pins, cardstock in multiple colors, beads, a shadow box of 9" x 9", and other baubles. This project has an intermediate level difficulty and should be done in two to three hours.

There are plenty of decorations you can make using these machines, whether it's for Christmas, Halloween, or other seasonal-themed decorations. Perhaps you are looking for something more permanent, like unique hanging planters. For this one, you will need any Cricut Explore Air or Maker, a deep cut blade, a standard grip mat, chipboard, foam brushes, a glue gun, DecoArt Acrylic parin, grey sky and sea glass, light masking tape and leather cording. Plus, you will need a plant (artificial one is better in this case), and a wire (but this is optional). If you choose the live plant, you will need a plastic recipient for soil and some small white gravel.

The fun part with project ideas is that what is trending today, may be already outdated tomorrow.

Ideas For "Professionally Design Crafts"

DIY Thank You Card With Gift Card Holder

Tweak this Thank You card with your preferred hues or your own decision of designed papers. Or on the other hand, go with the minimalist structure I've made utilizing simply hued Cricut pens and white cardstock. I have a Cricut Design Space canvas all set up and prepared for you to tweak and make. The card is structured with a little pocket, the perfect size for a standard gift voucher (or two). You can change the card size to meet your own requirements in the event that you'd like.

Make written by hand cards with your Cricut machine and Cricut pens.

Materials

• Cricut machine and Cricut Design Space

• White cardstock

• Multiple shaded Cricut Pens

• Glue

• Gift card of your decision.

343

Instructions

This card accompanies a coordinating envelope that you can discover in the project canvas. I've just made the card to exhibit this project.

1. Go to the project canvas in Cricut Design Space and adhere to on-screen guidelines to draw and cut the card.

2. Fold along the score lines and paste the gift voucher pocket set up.

3. Write a little note and give your blessing.

Lace Heart Paper Chain Valentine décor

Cricut Maker Decorate with a paper chain for San Valentine's Day. This chain of paper is delicately cut and piled together like hearts. Like lace doilies. The perfect decor for a holiday. Goes really good with the floral wreath of Valentine.

Materials

• Cricut Cardstock 12x24 Red Tones

• Cricut 12x12 Light Grip Mat

• This Lace Strip CDS project

• Stapler

• Cricut Maker

Instructions

• First, use Cricut Maker to cut the strips on a sensitive lace boundary strip. Cricut Cardstock 12x24 Red Tones.

• I've been using three red shades.

• Fold every strip in half afterward.

• Roll in a heart shape the top half of the strip.

• Then inside your heart, put the next folded piece.

• Stack together the four layers of paper.

• Repeat all paper strips of the process.

• Until a beautiful chain of heart paper is made.

• Put it on the entry table, or hang it like a garland.

• I love the lace look and heart forms. The decorative edge. The perfect day decoration for Valentine!

• Be good as often as you can.

Glass Etched Watercolor Wall Art

I am fond of the Hymn of "Scatter Sunshine," I love to see how the Sunshine is scattered along the way. The Hymn of "Scatter

Sunshine" It is a fun project to make a big gift or decorative piece, I love to etch things onto the glass.

You would need:

- Glass and frame

- Stewart Glass Etching Cream.

- Painters tape

- Vinyl cut out with positive space removed

Instructions

- I have used my Cricut Explore Air 2 to cut vinyl. Then use the vinyl and glass painter's tape.

- Use the etching cream and add the vinyl letters directly to the glass.

- Allow the cream for 15 minutes to sit on the glass. Then use a tool for removing the cream tool. You can put the cream in the bottle or discard it again.

- Wash off the cream and remove the vinyl fully with a damp cloth.

- Remove the etched lettering and reveal it.

- Now cut the frame's size of a piece of aquarelle paper. Add water loads and color touches.

- I've made a fun picture, using sunshine and sky colors.

- Let the aquarelle dry and put in the etching frame.

- Enjoy your hang up!

Shark Pencil Case: Return to Fun School!

The Craft Lightning: back to school edition is part of this project.

It takes 15 minutes to do this simple project, and it's perfect for SHARK week.

You would need:

- Cutting machine (having no one? Enter my Cricut Explore Air 2 gift here!)

- Felt

- Ball Chain Keychain

- Googly eyes

- Scissors

- Cutting machine

- Silver heat transfers, and iron

Instructions

• Upload the picture of the shark to your cutting software.

• Enter my Cricut Explore Air 2 gift here! I've been using my Cricut Air 2 Explorer.

• Simply cut the shark off the machine.

• Easy, take just a minute or two at any time.

• Excess vinyl is weeded out.

• Eye and gill slits included.

• Place on top of the box with the plastic.

• Slightly iron over the shark at the medium height.

• Nylon is the case, so if it gets too hot, it will melt.

• Then completely let it cool.

• Then peel the plastic off and roll it back over the top.

• All right, we're 5 minutes.

• Then take a felt piece and cut two identical bodies of fish. I modeled these gold-fish crackers slightly larger than cheesy. And I finished with two eyes googly (one on both sides).

• Stick on one fish hot ball chain keychain.

• Then add the other fish body right at the top, covering it with a chain. • (if the ball chain keychain is not lying around, use some yarn).

• Every side of the fish has a hot glue eye.

• Then crochet it as a cute shark snack to the zipper!

• Shark Bait

Ideas For "Other Paper Crafts"

Now that you know how to use the "Design Space" application to create unique designs and then cut them using one of the "Cricut" cutting machine. You are ready to start creating beautiful craft projects. So without further ado let's get you started!

Paper Projects

It is ideal to start your first project using paper-based designs, since these projects are easier to not only design but also to cut. You can get professional looking results with minimum investment. You will learn to create a variety of projects that you can further customize as you follow the instructions below and have unique designs of your own.

Recipe Stickers

Materials needed

- "Cricut Maker" or "Cricut Explore"
- Sticker paper and cutting mat.

Instructions

Step 1

Log into the "Design Space" application and click on the "New Project" button on the top right corner of the screen to view a blank canvas.

Step 2

Click on the "Images" icon on the "Design Panel" and type in "stickers" in the search bar. Click on desired image, then click on the "Insert Images" button at the bottom of the screen.

Step 3

The selected image will be displayed on the canvas and can be edited using applicable tools from the "Edit Image Bar". You can make multiple changes to the image as you need, for example, you could change the color of the image or change its size (sticker should be between 2-4 inches wide). The image selected for this project has words "stickers" inside the design, so let's delete that by first clicking on the "Ungroup" button and selecting the "Stickers" layer and clicking on the red "x" button.

Click on the "Text" button and type in the name of your recipe, as shown in the picture below.

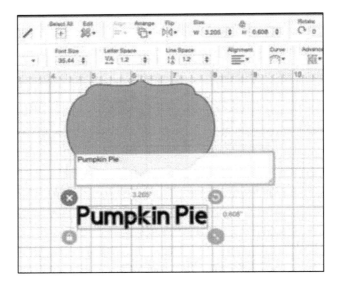

Step 4

Drag and drop the text in the middle of the design and select the entire design. Now, click on "Align" and select "Center Horizontally" and "Center Vertically".

Step 5

Select the entire design and click on "Group" icon on the top top right of the screen under "Layers panel". Now, copy and paste the designs and update the text for all your recipes.

Tip - Use your keyboard shortcut "Ctrl + C" and "Ctrl + V" to copy and paste the design.

Step 6

Click on "Save" at the top right corner of the screen to name and save your project.

Step 7

To cut your design, just click on the "Make It" button on the top right corner of the screen. Load the sticker paper to your "Cricut" machine and click "Continue" at the bottom right corner of the screen to start cutting your design.

Note – The "Continue" button will only appear after you have purchased images and fonts that are available for purchase only.

Step 8

Set your cut setting to "Vinyl" (recommended for sticker paper since it tends to be thicker than regular paper). Place the sticker paper on top of the cutting mat and follow the prompts on the screen to finish cutting your design. Viola! You have your own customized recipe stickers.

Wedding Invitations

Materials needed

- "Cricut Maker" or "Cricut Explore"
- Cutting mat
- Cardstock or your choice of decorative paper/ crepe paper/ fabric, home printer (if not using "Cricut Maker").

Instructions

Step 1

Log into the "Design Space" application and click on the "New Project" button on the top right corner of the screen to view a blank canvas.

Step 2

Let's customize an already existing project by clicking on the "Projects" icon on the "Design Panel" and selecting "Cards" from the "All Categories" drop-down then type in "wedding invite" in the search bar.

Step 3

For example, you could select the project shown in the picture below and click "Customize" at the bottom of the screen to edit and personalize the text of your invite.

Step 4

Click "Text" on the "Designs Panel" and type in the details of the invite. You can change the font, color and alignment of the text from the "Edit Text Bar" on top of the screen and remember to change the "Fill" to "Print" on the top of the screen.

355

Step 5

Select all the elements of the design and click on "Group" icon on the top right of the screen under "Layers panel". Then, click on "Save" to save your project

Step 6

Your design can now be printed and cut. Click on "Make It" button and follow the prompts on the screen to first print your design on your chosen material (white cardstock or paper) and subsequently cut the printed design.

Custom Notebooks

Materials needed

- "Cricut Maker" or "Cricut Explore"
- Cutting mat
- Washi sheets or your choice of decorative paper/ crepe paper/ fabric.

Instructions

Step 1

Log into the "Design Space" application and click on the "New Project" button on the top right corner of the screen to view a blank canvas.

356

Step 2

Using an already existing project from the "Cricut" library and customize it. So click on the "Projects" icon on the "Design Panel" and type in "notebook" in the search bar.

Step 3

Click on "Customize" so you can further edit the project to your preference. For example, the "unicorn notebook" project shown below. You can click on the "Linetype Swatch" to change the color of the design.

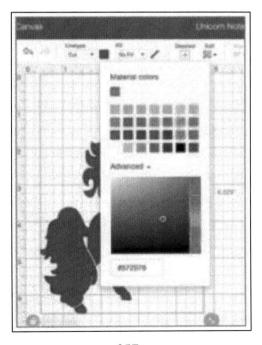

Step 4

The design is ready to be cut. Simply click on the "Make It" button and load the washi paper sheet to your "Cricut" machine and follow the instructions on the screen to cut your project.

Paper Flowers

Materials needed

- "Cricut Maker" or "Cricut Explore"
- Cutting Mat
- Cardstock
- Adhesive.

Instructions

Step 1

Log into the "Design Space" application and click on the "New Project" button on the top right corner of the screen to view a blank canvas.

Step 2

Click on the "Images" icon on the "Design Panel" and type in "flower" in the search bar. Click on desired image, then click on the "Insert Images" button at the bottom of the screen.

Step 3

The selected image will be displayed on the canvas and can be edited using applicable tools from the "Edit Image Bar". Then copy and paste the flower five times and make them a size smaller than the preceding flower to create variable size for depth and texture for the design, as shown in the picture below.

Step 4

The design is ready to be cut. Simply click on the "Make It" button and load the cardstock to your "Cricut" machine and follow the instructions on the screen to cut your project.

Step 5

Once the design has been cut, simply remove the cut flowers and bend them at the center. Then using the adhesive, stack the flowers with the largest flower at the bottom.

Crepe Paper Bouquet

Materials needed

- "Cricut Maker" or "Cricut Explore"
- Standardgrip mat
- Crepe paper in desired colors
- Floral wire
- Floral tape
- Hot glue
- Fern fronds
- Vase

Instructions

Step 1

Log into the "Design Space" application and click on the "New Project" button on the top right corner of the screen to view a blank canvas.

Step 2

Let's use an already existing project from the "Cricut" library and customize it. So click on the "Projects" icon and type in "crepe bouquet" in the search bar.

Step 3

Click on "Customize" so you can further edit the project to your preference or simply click on the "Make It" button and load the crepe paper to your "Cricut" machine and follow the instructions on the screen to cut your project.

Step 4

To assemble the design, follow the assembly instructions provided under the "Assemble" section of the project details, as shown in the picture below.

Leaf Banner

Materials needed

- "Cricut Maker" or "Cricut Explore"
- Standardgrip mat
- Watercolor paper and paint
- Felt balls
- Needle and thread
- Hot glue

Instructions

Step 1

Log into the "Design Space" application and click on the "New Project" button on the top right corner of the screen to view a blank canvas.

Step 2

Let's use an already existing project from the "Cricut" library and customize it. So click on the "Projects" icon and type in "leaf banner" in the search bar.

Step 3

Click on "Customize" so you can further edit the project to your preference or simply click on the "Make It" button and load the

363

watercolor paper to your "Cricut" machine and follow the instructions on the screen to cut your project.

Step 4

Use watercolors to paint the leaves and let them dry completely. Then create a garland using the needle and thread through the felt balls and sticking the leaves to the garland with hot glue.

Paper Pinwheels

Materials needed

- "Cricut Maker" or "Cricut Explore"
- Standardgrip mat
- Patterned cardstock in desired colors
- Embellishments
- Paper straws
- Hot glue

Instructions

Step 1

Log into the "Design Space" application and click on the "New Project" button on the top right corner of the screen to view a blank canvas.

Step 2

Let's use an already existing project from the "Cricut" library and customize it. So click on the "Projects" icon and type in "paper pinwheel" in the search bar.

Step 3

Click on "Customize" to further edit the project to your preference or simply click on the "Make It" button and load the cardstock to your "Cricut" machine and follow the instructions on the screen to cut your project.

Step 4

Using hot glue, adhere the pinwheels together to the paper straws and the embellishment, as shown in the picture below.

Paper Lollipops

Materials needed

- "Cricut Maker" or "Cricut Explore"
- Lightgrip mat
- Patterned cardstock in desired colors
- Glitter
- Wooden dowels
- Hot glue

Instructions

Step 1

Log into the "Design Space" application and click on the "New Project" button on the top right corner of the screen to view a blank canvas.

Step 2

Let's use an already existing project from the "Cricut" library and customize it. So click on the "Projects" icon and type in "paper lollipop" in the search bar.

Step 3

Click on "Customize" to further edit the project to your preference or simply click on the "Make It" button and load the cardstock to your "Cricut" machine and follow the instructions on the screen to cut your project.

Step 4

Using hot glue adhere the down between the lollipop circles. Brush them with craft glue and sprinkle with glitter.

Paper Luminary

Materials needed

- "Cricut Maker" or "Cricut Explore"
- Standardgrip mat
- Shimmer paper sampler
- Weeder
- Spray adhesive

- Frosted glass luminary

Instructions

Step 1

Log into the "Design Space" application and click on the "New Project" button on the top right corner of the screen to view a blank canvas.

Step 2

Let's use an already existing project from the "Cricut" library and customize it. So click on the "Projects" icon and type in "paper luminary" in the search bar.

Step 3

Click on "Customize" to further edit the project to your preference or simply click on the "Make It" button and load the shimmer paper to your "Cricut" machine and follow the instructions on the screen to cut your project.

Step 4

Cut and weed the design then spray the back of the shimmer paper with spray adhesive and adhere to the glass luminary, as shown in the picture below.

Ideas For "Iron-On Projects"

DIY Cricut on Iron-on vinyl on Fabric bodysuit

Iron-on vinyl is a special type of vinyl material with heat adhesives properties that can be used easily with other materials fabric, wood, or paper.

Vinyl is classified into two types, which are adhesive vinyl and iron-on vinyl. The sample project details will show how to use Cricut iron-on vinyl on bodysuits.

Supplies for Cricut iron-on vinyl project on bodysuits

Bodysuit or any other material of your preference, depending on your project

Cricut iron-on vinyl

- Weeding tool
- Cricut EasyPress or household iron
- Cricut files for the bodysuit project
- A scrap of fabric
- Standard grip mat or a light blue grip mat

Directions on how to cut iron-on vinyl

- First, start by opening the Cricut Design Space, then go to the library to select preferred images. On the left side of the design panel, click "images." Go to the search bar at the upper right to search for images.

- Once the images you search for are on your canvas, you can now resize them using the edit toolbar at the top corner.

Hints

While searching on the Design Space, always endeavor to put the # sign for easy search. Also, note that you can also use templates in Cricut design space to help in resizing your images.

- The next step is to go Color Sync panel and drag all your images there to be the same color. This will enable your project to cut on the same mat in your Cricut machine.

- Then click the "make it" icon at the top of your canvas.

Hint

Always make sure you select "mirror" in the sidebar of the canvas to flip your image. This will allow your image not to go back when you're about to iron it on.

- The next step is to click "Continue."

- On your Cricut machine, set the dial under material settings to iron-on.

- On the cutting mat, place the plastic iron vinyl side down.

Hint

You can use the tool Cricut Bayer to help press firmly the vinyl into the cutting mat.

- The next step is to insert the cutting mat into the Cricut machine and then press the arrow button on the Cricut machine. This will immediately grip the cutting mat to the machine.

- Press the "C" button. It will begin to cut your project.

- Once the machine is done cutting your project. Press the arrow button, and it will release the cutting mat for removal.

DIY on How to Weed Cricut Iron-on Vinyl on Projects

Weeding during your project is the process of removing anything or leftovers that are not part of your design.

To have an effective weeding, you start by digging the tip of your weeding tool into the piece of the vinyl that is not part of your design and carefully peel it off.

After weeding, if you flip your material, you will notice your design is facing the right way. But if you forgot to mirror it on the canvas, all the design will be backward, that is spoiling all the design process.

- Finally, always double-check to ensure you do not have any leftover on the vinyl that needs weeding.

Tips and Tricks that make weeding on your iron-on easy

One major step between cutting and ironing during your project is weeding your vinyl. The following tips will help you to weed your vinyl in a more relaxed fashion.

Use other tools for an effective result- You can always use different weeding tools for any type of weeding in different situations. A needle, straight pin, or a pair of tweezers will be useful to weed off vinyl in thinnest areas. Other tools can be right as well for different weeding jobs like a craft knife.

Print out your project design- If your project is an intricate design, it will be ideal for printing it out before weeding. This will enable you to see clearly what needs to be removed or what exactly is the part of the design.

Find a hook that works for your project- Cricut has many weeding tools that have several hooks you can choose from. There are some weeding hooks in the market, but the Cricut weeding hook tends to be the favorite among crafters. Other brands come with different shapes and sizes, find the ones that work for your project.

Keep your project material on the Cricut mat-You will find the weeding easy if your material is stuck to the cutting mat. This will hold down the material while you weed the vinyl.

Make use of Cricut Brightpad- If you are having difficulty in seeing the weeding lines during your weeding process, get a Cricut bright pad. This tool is a thin lightbox that you can weed your vinyl on. This tool shines through the thin weed lines and makes it easier to weed.

Go slowly during the weeding process- Always take it slowly and carefully when weeding your vinyl. Some iron-on vinyl tends to weed more quickly than others.

DIY on How to Fix the Cricut Iron-on Vinyl

There are three ways you can adhere to iron-on vinyl during your cutting project. The three types of heat sources are household iron, heat press, and Cricut EasyPress.

Household iron method with Iron-on vinyl

Set your iron to the highest heat with zero steam because iron-on does not work very well with steam. Before you place the design on your bodysuit, make sure you do a pre-press with the iron for about 5 seconds. The advantage of this pre-press is to let the bodysuit flatten and quickens the adhesion process when it starts.

During your adhesion, you can iron directly on the plastic or use a scrap of cloth on top of the plastic sheet.

Cricut EasyPress with Iron-on vinyl

There are different sizes of Cricut EasyPress, but the common one for household usage among crafters is the Cricut EasyPress 2. Likewise, the household iron, pre-press the bodysuit to flattens and starts the adhesion process when you add your design.

- Press down the Cricut Easypress with steady pressure on the bodysuit and press on the "C" button. The Cricut Easypress will count to 30 seconds for the adhesion. Likewise, adhering vinyl with the iron let the iron-on on the bodysuit cool down a bit before you peel back the plastic carrier sheet.

375

Iron-on vinyl with Heat press.

This process is somewhat similar to the other two types, except you will be using a giant heating machine.

- During the adhesion process, set your heat press to 315 degrees and 15 seconds. Also, like others, do a pre-press with the heat like five seconds. Then add your design to the bodysuit, and with the heat press machine, you are going to be using Teflon pressing sheet to aid this process. Let the iron-on cool before you start to peel back the plastic layer from the bodysuit.

Hint

The processes mentioned above are the three different ways you can use Cricut iron-on vinyl or any other type of vinyl. Regardless of any kind of heat source you use, always make sure you wait for 24 hours before wash. This helps you to preserve the design of the bodysuit.

DIY Iron-on Vinyl on Wood Design

The two types of vinyl—iron-on and adhesive vinyl can be used for wood design. Still, the iron-on vinyl is perfect for wood design because the wood surface is rough, and it takes a significant amount of effort before the vinyl stick to its cover of the wood.

However, iron-on tends to adhere perfectly to the wood surface, and you do not need a transfer tape because the vinyl complies entirely with the transfer sheet.

Supplies for wood design

- Iron-on vinyl
- Wood plaque
- Weeding tool
- Design Cricut space file
- Cricut EasyPress

Directions to create an iron-on wood design

- The first step is to download the SVG file or create your preferred design on the Cricut Design Space.

- Set the Cricut machine dial to iron-on.

- Make sure you mirror the image.

- Before you send the design to the machine to cut, endeavor to place the iron-on vinyl on the cutting mat.

- Cut the file or design on your Cricut machine.

- Once the Cricut machine is finished cutting, weed out the excess vinyl.

If you mirror your image in the Cricut design space, you will see that your image is backward, but when you flip it on the wood, it will show up the right way.

- The next step is to turn on your Cricut Easypress and set the dial to the right setting for wood on the vinyl project; the standard environment for the most wood project is 300 degrees and 40 seconds.

- Then firmly press down your Cricut EasyPress to the wood.

Hint

You can use a piece of cotton fabric between the Cricut EasyPress and the vinyl. This helps you to move the Cricut EasyPress around quickly, making sure you capture all the parts of your transfer design. Also, note that you can do additional press if the vinyl didn't adhere properly to the wood.

- Gently peel off the back plastic from the wood.

This is the process to take in adhering vinyl to wood, and you can use this technique for various projects relating to wood.

DIY a Banner with Iron-on Vinyl on Cardstock

Out of all the primary materials you can use iron-on vinyl with, paper and cardstock are the most inexpensive of them all—and you can create a beautiful project with them.

The following steps will show you how to use vinyl on cardstock by creating a banner that can be used for engagements, as gifts, weddings, and parties.

Supplies for Banner

- Cricut Easypress or household iron
- A white cardstock
- A gold glitter iron-on vinyl
- A ribbon

Directions of using iron-on on cardstock to create a banner

- Download banner SVG cut file. And you can design your banner file or upload the downloaded file to Cricut Design Space.

Hint

Note that the banner file usually comes with a measurement of 5 inches x 7 inches, but you can resize it to your preference. Do not forget to mirror your iron-on vinyl so that your letters will face the right direction when you iron them to your cardstock or any other material.

- Once the Cricut machine has cut your cardstock and glitter iron, then you can weed out the negative area from the iron-on vinyl.

- Line up all the iron-on pieces over the cardstock pans. You can use household iron or Cricut EasyPress to press the vinyl to the cardstock.

Hint

For cardstock, low heat is required for adhesion. Press for a minimum of 30 seconds and flip to press for 15 seconds from the back.

- Peel off the plastic liner after the heat press and keep the paper from curling by placing them under heavy object like a book.

- Use ribbon to string together your newly made banner pieces.

Ideas For "Vinyl"

Vinyl is one of the most common supplies to use with Cricut machines, no matter which one you have. The Cricut Explore One, Cricut Explore Air 2, and Cricut Maker all easily cut through vinyl. The Cricut EasyPress makes using heat transfer vinyl incredibly easy. Vinyl can serve as the design itself, a removable sticker, or a stencil. These ten projects were chosen to cover a wide range of methods and different types of vinyl. Feel free to follow the instructions exactly, or change the types of materials listed.

There are several different types of vinyl. Most of the projects specify which vinyl to use, but you could use different ones depending on the use of the object. The four basic categories that all vinyl falls under are permanent, removable, iron-on (or heat transfer vinyl), and window cling. Permanent vinyl is designed to last and is good for outdoor projects, projects that are going to get a lot of handling, and projects you'll want to be able to wash. Removable vinyl is just that. It's adhesive and can be removed again. It's not suited for outdoor use or heavy handling. It's often used for stencils or temporary stickers. A heat transfer vinyl transfers to a surface using heat and pressure from something like an iron or a Cricut EasyPress. Finally, window cling is another type of vinyl with temporary use, but it's not actually adhesive. It uses static to adhere to glass or other very smooth surfaces.

Cricut offers a wide variety of vinyl types. They have different colors and patterns, shimmer, glitter, holographic, glossy, dry erase, chalkboard, printable, and stencil vinyl. For the most part, whatever you get will come down to personal preference and what you want to use it for. However, some may only be available in permanent, temporary, or is otherwise limited. The best thing to do is search by the usage first, then choose a color and finish from that listing.

Vinyl transfer tape is a crucial component no matter what type of vinyl you are using. If you are shopping Cricut brand, they offer regular and Strong Grip transfer tape. The Strong Grip is for tougher vinyl, such as glitter.

If you are buying different brands of vinyl, they will often come with transfer tape to use with them. If they don't, you should be able to find it separately at the same store.

Treasure Chest Jewelry Box

Turn a simple wooden box into a treasure chest! This is a cute project for yourself or your child. Choose the type of wooden box you like best. You can find one with flat or rounded lids and in all different sizes. You could get one that's already in the color you like, a light color to stain or paint yourself, or even an older box that looks like it could be a treasure chest. White vinyl is a good basic that will show up on any wood, but you could change the color depending on how you want your box to look. Scale this up to create a toy or storage box. You can use the Cricut Explore One, Cricut Explore Air 2, or Cricut Maker for this project.

- Supplies Needed

- Plain wooden box with lid
- White vinyl
- Vinyl transfer tape
- Cutting mat
- Weeding tool or pick
- Small blade

Instructions

- Open Cricut Design Space and create a new project.
- Select the "Image" button in the lower left-hand corner and search for "keyhole."
- Click your favorite keyhole design and click "Insert."
- Select the "Text" button in the lower left-hand corner.
- Choose your favorite font and type "Treasure."
- Place your vinyl on the cutting mat.
- Send the design to your Cricut.
- Use a weeding tool or pick to remove the excess vinyl from the design.
- Apply separate pieces of transfer tape to the keyhole and the word.
- Remove the paper backing from the tape on the keyhole.
- Place the keyhole where the lid and box meet so that half is on the lid and half is on the box.

384

- Rub the tape to transfer the vinyl to the wood, making sure there are no bubbles. Carefully peel the tape away.
- Use a sharp blade to cut the keyhole design in half so that the box can open.
- Transfer the word to the front of the box using the same method.
- Optional: Add details with paint or markers to make the box look more like a treasure chest. Add wood grain, barnacles, seashells, or pearls.
- Store your jewelry in your new treasure chest!

Motivational Water Bottle

Everyone needs a motivational boost to keep their workouts going. Turn a boring water bottle into your personal cheerleader! Choose the type of water bottle that you like the best, whether it's a plastic, glass, or metal one. This could also work on a reusable tumbler if you prefer to have a straw. The glitter vinyl will give a fun accent to your necessary hydration, but you can change it to a regular color if you want to be a bit less flashy. Use one of the suggested quotes or one of your own. The important thing is that it motivates you to keep moving! You can use the

Cricut Explore One, Cricut Explore Air 2, or Cricut Maker for this project.

Supplies Needed

- Sturdy water bottle of your choice
- Glitter vinyl
- Vinyl transfer tape
- Light grip cutting mat
- Weeding tool or pick

Instructions

- Open Cricut Design Space and create a new project.
- Measure the space on your water bottle where you want the text, and create a box that size.
- Select the "Text" button in the lower left-hand corner.
- Choose your favorite font, and type the motivational quote you like best.
- I sweat glitter
- Sweat is magic
- I don't sweat, I sparkle
- Place your vinyl on the cutting mat.
- Send the design to your Cricut.
- Use a weeding tool or pick to remove the excess vinyl from the text.

387

- Apply transfer tape to the quote.

- Remove the paper backing from the tape.

- Place the quote where you want it on the water bottle.

- Rub the tape to transfer the vinyl to the bottle, making sure there are no bubbles. Carefully peel the tape away.

- Bring your new water bottle to the gym for motivation and hydration!

Customized Makeup Bag

Bathroom counter a mess from all your makeup? Make yourself a cute bag to store it in! This can be any size bag or pouch you'd like, from one that holds a few items to a train case. The only requirement is enough blank space for the design. Pink and purple create a classic, feminine look, but you can use whatever color combination suits you best. This is the first project using heat transfer vinyl, so you'll need a Cricut EasyPress or iron to transfer the design onto the bag. You can use the Cricut Explore One, Cricut Explore Air 2, or Cricut Maker for this project.

Supplies Needed

- Pink fabric makeup bag
- Purple heat transfer vinyl
- Cricut EasyPress or iron
- Cutting mat
- Weeding tool or pick
- Keychain or charm of your choice

Instructions

- Open Cricut Design Space and create a new project.
- Measure the space on your makeup bag where you want the design, and create a box that size.
- Select the "Image" button in the lower left-hand corner and search "monogram."
- Choose your favorite monogram and click "Insert."
- Place your vinyl on the cutting mat.
- Send the design to your Cricut.

389

- Use a weeding tool or pick to remove the excess vinyl from the design.
- Place the design on the bag with the plastic side up.
- Carefully iron on the design.
- After cooling, peel away the plastic by rolling it.
- Hang your charm or keychain off the zipper.
- Stash your makeup in your customized bag!

Perpetual Calendar

Woodblock calendars are a cute addition to any décor. Many teachers use them on their desks, or they fit in anywhere in your home. You can find unfinished block calendars online or at most craft stores. They'll usually have two wooden cubes for the numbers, two longer blocks for the months, and a stand to hold them. Painting the wood will give you the color of your choice, but you could also stain it or look around for calendars made of different types of wood. You can use the Cricut Explore One, Cricut Explore Air 2, or Cricut Maker for this project.

Supplies Needed

- Unfinished woodblock calendar
- Acrylic paint in color(s) of your choosing.
- Vinyl color(s) of your choosing
- Vinyl transfer tape
- Cutting mat
- Weeding tool or pick
- Mod Podge

Instructions

- Paint the woodblock calendar in the colors you'd like and set aside to dry.
- Open Cricut Design Space, and create a new project.
- Create a square the correct size for the four blocks.
- Select the "Text" button in the lower left-hand corner.

- Choose your favorite font, and type the following numbers as well as all of the months: 0, 0, 1, 1, 2, 2, 3, 4, 5, 6, 7, 8
- Place your vinyl on the cutting mat.
- Send the design to your Cricut.
- Use a weeding tool or pick to remove the excess vinyl from the text.
- Apply transfer tape to each separate number and the months.
- Remove the paper backing from the tape, and apply the numbers as follows.
- 0 and 5 on the top and bottom of the first block
- 1, 2, 3, 4 around the sides of the first block
- 0 and 8 on the top and bottom of the second block
- 1, 2, 6, 7 around the sides of the second block
- Remove the paper backing from the tape on the months, and apply them to the long blocks, the first six months on one and the second six months on the other.
- Rub the tape to transfer the vinyl to the wood, making sure there are no bubbles. Carefully peel the tape away.
- Seal everything with a coat of Mod Podge.
- Arrange your calendar to display today's date, and enjoy it year after year!

Wooden Gift Tags

Dress up your gifts with special wooden tags! Balsa wood is light and easy to cut. The wood tags with gold names will give all of your gifts a shabby chic charm. Change up the color of the vinyl as you see fit; you can even use different colors for different gift recipients. People will be able to keep these tags and use them for something else, as well. An alternative to balsa wood is chipboard, though it won't have the same look. The Cricut Maker is the best choice for this project, though the Cricut Explore One and Cricut Explore Air 2 can get by using the Deep Cut Blade.

Supplies Needed

- Balsa wood
- Gold vinyl
- Vinyl transfer tape
- Cutting mat

- Weeding tool or pick

Instructions

- Secure your small balsa wood pieces to the cutting mat, then tape the edges with masking tape for additional strength.
- Open Cricut Design Space and create a new project.
- Select the shape you would like for your tags and set the Cricut to cut wood, then send the design to the Cricut.
- Remove your wood tags from the Cricut and remove any excess wood.
- In Cricut Design Space, select the "Text" button in the lower left-hand corner.
- Choose your favorite font, and type the names you want to place on your gift tags.
- Place your vinyl on the cutting mat.
- Send the design to your Cricut.
- Use a weeding tool or pick to remove the excess vinyl from the text.
- Apply transfer tape to the quote.
- Remove the paper backing from the tape.
- Place the names on the wood tags.
- Rub the tape to transfer the vinyl to the wood, making sure there are no bubbles. Carefully peel the tape away.

- Thread twine or string through the holes, and decorate your gifts!

Pet Mug

Show your love for your pet every morning when you have your coffee! A cute silhouette of a cat or dog with some paw prints is a simple but classy design. You're not limited to those two animals, either. Use a bird with bird footprints, a fish with water drops, or whatever pet you might have! You can add your pet's name or a quote to the design as well. You have the freedom here to arrange the aspects of the design however you'd like. You could put the animal in the center surrounded by the paw prints, scatter the prints all around the mug, place the animal next to its name and paw prints along the top, or whatever else you can imagine. Think of this as a tribute to your favorite pet or dedication to your favorite animal, and decorate accordingly. You can use the Cricut Explore One, Cricut Explore Air 2, or Cricut Maker for this project.

Supplies Needed

- Plain white mug
- Glitter vinyl
- Vinyl transfer tape
- Cutting mat
- Weeding tool or pick

Instructions

- Open Cricut Design Space and create a new project.
- Select the "Image" button in the lower left-hand corner and search for "cat," "dog," or any other pet of your choice.
- Choose your favorite image and click "Insert."

- Search images again for paw prints, and insert into your design.
- Arrange the pet and paw prints how you'd like them on the mug.
- Place your vinyl on the cutting mat.
- Send the design to your Cricut.
- Use a weeding tool or pick to remove the excess vinyl from the design.
- Apply transfer tape to the design.
- Remove the paper backing, and apply the design to the mug.
- Rub the tape to transfer the vinyl to the mug, making sure there are no bubbles. Carefully peel the tape away.
- Enjoy your custom pet mug!

Organized Toy Bins

How much of a mess is your kids' room? We already know the answer to that. Grab some plastic bins and label them with different toy categories, and teach your child to sort! You can use the type of bins that suit your child or their room best. Many people like to use the ones that look like giant buckets with handles on the sides. There are also more simple square ones. You could even use cheaper laundry baskets or plastic totes with or without the lids. Once your child is old enough to read the labels, it will be easier for them to put away toys and find them again to play. You can add images to the designs as well— whatever will make your child like them best! You can use the

Cricut Explore One, Cricut Explore Air 2, or Cricut Maker for this project.

Supplies Needed

- Plastic toy bins in colors of your choice
- White vinyl
- Vinyl transfer tape
- Cutting mat
- Weeding tool or pick

Instructions

- Open Cricut Design Space and create a new project.
- Select the "Text" button in the lower left-hand corner.
- Choose your favorite font and type the labels for each toy bin. See below for some possibilities.

    Legos

    Dolls

    Cars

    Stuffed animals

    Outside Toys

- Place your vinyl on the cutting mat.
- Send the design to your Cricut.
- Use a weeding tool or pick to remove the excess vinyl from the text.

399

- Apply transfer tape to the words.
- Remove the paper backing and apply the design to the bin.
- Rub the tape to transfer the vinyl to the bin, making sure there are no bubbles. Carefully peel the tape away.
- Organize your kid's toys in your new bins!

Froggy Rain Gear

Kids love to play outside in the rain. It can be hard to get them to dress properly for it, though. Decorate a raincoat and rain boots

with a cute froggy design that will have them asking to wear them! A simple raincoat and boots that you can find at any store for a reasonable price become custom pieces with this project. The outdoor vinyl is made to withstand the elements and last for ages. You can customize this even more by adding your child's name or change up the theme completely with different images. You can use the Cricut Explore One, Cricut Explore Air 2, or Cricut Maker for this project.

Supplies Needed

- Matching green raincoat and rain boots
- White outdoor vinyl
- Vinyl transfer tape
- Cutting mat
- Weeding tool or pick

Instructions

- Open Cricut Design Space and create a new project.
- Select the "Image" button in the lower left-hand corner and search for "frog."
- Choose your favorite frog and click "Insert."
- Copy the frog and resize. You will need three frogs, a larger one for the coat and two smaller ones for each boot.

- Place your vinyl on the cutting mat.
- Send the design to your Cricut.
- Use a weeding tool or pick to remove the excess vinyl from the design.
- Apply transfer tape to the design.
- Remove the paper backing and apply the design to the coat or boot.
- Rub the tape to transfer the vinyl to the rain gear, making sure there are no bubbles. Carefully peel the tape away.
- Dress your kid up to play in the rain!

Ideas For "Synthetic Leather Design"

Cactus Faux Leather Cricut Tote Bag!

Polka dot plants made from Cricut Creator, Iron on EasyPress and Cactus on faux leather tote bag! Is this bag not the perfect cactus tote?! It's easy to make many times with a simple picture break. The best thing to do is to apply Iron-on Vinyl to fake leather perfectly and it couldn't be easier!

You would need:

• Cricut maker or cutting machine

• Green Feather Iron on Vinyl

• EasyPress 2 thin

• Cricut Iron on Protective pad

• Cricut Design Space Instructions cactus

Instructions

- Place the iron on the side of the mat in color vinyl down to cut it.
- Weed out excess plastic, cool 14 cactus.

403

- I love the bright iron foil! Cut off all the cacti.
- Then inside the fake leather tote placed the EasyPress pad.
- Line the cactus to know the distance for the finished product you want. The first one or three is then mounted.
- The protective surface should be sealed.
- Set the EasyPress 2 to the proper false leather configuration. It can be slightly cooler at 295 to keep the tote from melting and squeezed at once for five seconds. Then another five seconds pulled.
- Tap on the EasyPress firmly.
- Repeat for every cacti cluster.
- Let the vinyl completely cool down and then remove plastic sheet from the container.
- Simple, when cooled down, to peel off. Re-press if necessary if it doesn't look like it is adhered to.
- Now the bag is ready to fill and remove from the city with all kinds of goodies. It's also a great homemade gift!

The Pen Holder Clasp Mini Leather Journal with Cricut Maker

First of all, for everyone on your list, you can make great gifts. My favorite are handmade gifts... but I want to ensure that they're of the highest standards. The manufacturer is incredible, because she can cut fabric, wood, leather, falsifying leather, chipboard etc.! Here's a great project I've developed, and I'm giving you free – Merry Christmas.

You would need:

• Cricut Iron-on Foil

• Cricut EasyPress 2 Small

• Cricut EasyPress Mat

• Cricut Bright Pad

• Cricut Essential Tool

• Cricut Iron-On Patent Protection

• Mini Composition Book

• Rubber Cement Glue

• This Cricut Design Space Project

Instructions

- Cricut Design Space opens this project
- Place the faux pebble leather on the Cricut mat. It's all ready to go and doesn't need to mirror the project.
- Slide in the mat and place in the holder the marking wheel. The first result of the project will be.
- Then remove a marker, and replace it with the fine blade. During this process do not remove the mat. Simply replace the blade and press C.
- You can cut out the forms fast, and remove them from the mat.
- Cut a few vinyl pictures out of iron. The pictures need only be 1.75 cm or less.
- Heat up to 300* your EasyPress 2 and place the iron-on journal cover on the EasyPress mat.
- Cover and press EasyPress 2 15 seconds. Cover with protection plate. This is it! This is it!
- Let the iron-on refresh fully... the carrier sheet then flake back.
- The time for cement rubber now.

- Cut a faux leather scrap piece that covers the diary slits. Add the backside of the diary and the top side of the piece cut with rubber cement... do not put the slit on the piece.
- Dry the cement rubber and cover the smaller piece with the slits.
- Then put the cement on the top of the diary book and the cover of the inside of it. Tacky, let them dry.
- Press the rubber cement book of the leather and then line up and press. Apply rubber cement to the back of the book and leather inside. No cement rubber between the lines scored. Allow the rubber cement to dry and then pick and press.
- Press firmly down to secure your book. The book will remain perfect until you have a new book of fillers to peel and glue off. Leather can be used again in this way!
- Please fold over the top flap and insert in a slit loop a mini pen or a regular pen. It makes the journal's perfect fastening! Never sit down without a pen for writing or sketching.

- This project only takes 15 minutes when Cricut Maker is set up and ready to go. That's the best handmade donation or stocking cushion!

Leather Foil Iron-on Name Gift Tag Cricut Maker's Keychains!

The Cricut Maker is incredible... totally one step up from the awesome Explore Air 2. If you're in the machine market... get the Maker, or you'll want to do it every time. The Maker can do stuff no other machine could have done before. The Cricut Maker is a major investment but the amount it can make is limitless! It has extra pressure so that it can use knife blades, scores or rotary blades, all of which are major game changers. Each day of the week, I use my Cricut. Make gifts, save time, make everything. The Cricut Maker has so many more options and thus much more ways (if it is your business). If you're a newbie, the Maker Spring—or you'll always want to. You start with Paper and Vinyl and then move quickly to iron-on and more. The learning curve is fast. You're going to want to cut textile, board, chipboard, leather in no time... you want to scoring paper and cut patterns in fabric. Get the Cricut Maker so that you have space to develop.

Let me show you how easy it is to make these honeymoon keys... perfect for gift tags that can be used in zip pulls, keychains, baggage tags, etc.

You will need:

- Cricut Iron-on Foil in rose gold

- Cricut EasyPress 2 Small

- Cricut EasyPress Mat

- Cricut Bright Pad

- Cricut Essential Tools

- Cricut True Control Knife

- Cricut Self-Healing Mat

- Keychain Lanyards

- Cricut Normal and Strong Grip Cutting

- Cricut Self-Healing Cutting Mat

- Cricut EasyPress 2 Small

- Cricut EasyPress Mat

- Criciut EasyPress

Instructions

- Start by opening up Cricut Design Space
- Design Space comes complete with many font, pictures and characteristics so that it can be used immediately after you plug into it. You can easily upload your own images, but the project today will only use a Cricut fountain.
- Create and open a textbox to a new canvas. Specify your name, and in the drop-down list, select the ZOO DAY font. The all-cap fonts are perfect for this. It works great. When the name has been written down, the letter space is decreased so that the letters start to touch each other. Touch them before and after each letter.
- You can check out my project here, but your own custom names must be created.
- Make it visible to both layers.
- Changing the iron-on vinyl color from the top layer to the color... or closing.
- Double every name now.
- The background of one version must be visible, the other the front.
- Select and solder every single name. All letters will be merged into one solid piece.

410

- After soldering, the background is solid and each name is solid. Choose and sweat or join all the blue names. Repeat the yellow names soldering.
- Click on the button to make it.
- On two separate mats you will bring up the sold or attached words.
- Mirror the front-end mat picture. Then, with a glittering side, place the iron-on vinyl on your mat. Set the Iron-on Foil configuration of the machine.
- Click on the "C" button and insert it into the Cricut Maker. It will cut the picture with the fine dot blade beautifully.
- Remove the vinyl iron and trim the edges once cut. Set it above your Bright Pad Cricut and see where you should weed. It has a breeze. To remove excess vinyl, use the weeding tool.
- Get the leather ready for the second mat. Leather cutting was never so easy with the Blade and the Builder Knife.
- To help protect your cutting mat against leather, use the contact paper. Remove the leather packaging and turn it roughly onto it.

- Place the paper and securely paste it on clear contact paper. Cut the leather in plastic.
- Slide onto the machine and put the chrome blade in the machine to the right.
- Make certain you have calibrated the blade beforehand.
- Put the leather-covered contact paper right on the strong grip mat.
- Place the blade in the Cricut Maker and have a chrome blade easily cut the leather.

Rose Gold Leather Earrings DIY

With a Cricut Maker you can do so many incredible things! Some honeymoon earrings only take a few minutes to make. The earrings of the leather are perfect because they can be very large, but they are lightweight and wear comfortable. These golden roses are great!

Make a fast pair of earrings for a gift, for wear and fun, and make a bunch for sale!

Supplies Required:

• Cricut Maker

- Cricut Strong Grip Mat

- Clear Contact Paper

- Cricut Metalic Rose Gold Vinyl

- Cricuts tools

- Hook and jump rings

- Criticut Metal leather Gold Cricut

Instructions

- Start by stitching a clear contact paper to the back side of the leather. This keeps everything from the matt surface and keeps the mat more useful. Place the leather on the strong grip mat (contact paper side down).

- To design a rope shape with a tiny hole cut at the top, use Cricut Design Space. Cut it off, then. I shouted I was using the blade for the knife, but I was too tired to switch to it.

- And the leather wasn't really cut all around its rear edge, so there's a bit of fluff. I cut it off with the scissors of Cricut.

- Then use some pins to attach a hook on the leather earring.

413

- Cut some sweet shapes out of metallic rose vinyl gold. These are the forms in the Cricut Access file I found on a CDS.
- Then peel the leather and stick it to the back. The rose-gold and rose-gold vinyl go hand in hand.
- Under the layers of leather, I like the hit metallic.
- Such a simple DIY for a good declaration pair of earrings.

Paper Ferens Resin Serving Tray DIY

I love the trendy, tropical atmosphere right now; it makes me dream of the days on a sandy beach with palm trees and light blue skies. I love the trendy tropical atmosphere. I'm going to have to settle down for this tropical tray breakfast in bed. This box is easy to make and uses resin, my favorite medium!

It's also a great handmade gift! Ideal for serving breakfast in bed on Mother's Day or Father's Day!

Supplies Required

• Bamboo service tray

- High-gloss Envirotex Lite resin

- Green shade paper

- Ultra seal

- Cricut explorer Air 2 machine

- White paint

- Resin instruction manual handles, cups and sticks

Instructions

- Start with paint inside the tray.
- Cut the leafy ferns into 3 colors of green paper during drying on the tray.
- Sufficient ferns and fronds should be available to fill the tray.
- Then make straight lines on the blades with a straight edge and cutter.
- It fits snugly on the tray's edges.
- Once cut and fit on the tray, cover with the Ultra Seal the bottom of the tray, then place the leaves above and cover the top with additional Ultra Seal. It can slightly bubble up. Don't be panic. Don't panic. Completely let it dry.

415

- Prepare now your resin surface for work. Lite Pour-on High Gloss Finish I love Environtex! It turns whatever you create into a business piece!
- Mix the resin to the instructions of the package.
- Then pour directly into the middle of the tray.
- Tilt the tray slightly to cover the whole base of the tray with the resin. Twenty minutes let it sit. Then use a butane torch or a heat pistol to pop any of the forming bubbles. Then cover with a card piece and let it heal overnight.
- It's ready to use when the tray doesn't smell like resin!
- Filler with a delicious breakfast, or use on the couch as a work surface. There are many ways to experience this fun tropical tray.

Gold Foil Rose Iron-On Vinyl on Cricut Straw Bag!

Make a fancy bag with some rose gold foil even a fancier. It's a dumbbell and it takes only a few minutes to make a fantastic handmade present. Have you a bag around which a boost can be used? If you're anything like me, maybe more than one!

You are going to need

- Cricut EasyPress 2

- Cricut EasyPress

- Rose Gold Foil Iron-on Vinyl

- Cricut Maker

- Cricut EasyPress Mat

Instructions

- I bought that flower design from Cricut Design Space by searching for the' flower'— the bag that needs update. Place the rose gold sheet on the mat with the shiny gold surface on the tile, look over the picture. Then cut the shape off in the right place. Excess vinyl should be removed and weeded.

- Set it on the top of the bag with a bright side. Remain firm while it presses inside the bag with towels.

- Cover with a cover or teflon board to prevent melting of the bag.

- Set the EasyPress 2 at the correct material temperature. Pull down firmly while heating (Check this chart).
- Let the project fully refresh before the carrier plate is removed.
- The bag is now ready to be gifted or filled!

Ideas For "Wooden Designs"

Before delving into this project, I would like to explain a few important tips for this project that will help you complete the task accurately. Go over them as much as you can in order to fully understand each of these tips. It will definitely help you.

Do not eject the mat when you pause the machine to clean or replace a blunt rotary blade. If you remove the mat, it will be difficult the get the correct alignment of the cut and finish your project with accuracy. So, what you do is to pause the machine, remove the rotary blade, clean or replace the rotary blade, put it back in and hit the Cricut button to continue. You will have to do all these without ejecting the mat.

Before you unload your material from the machine, ensure that you check your project and that the cut was done all the way. If the cut is not all the way, you can restart the cut all over again as long as you did not eject or move the mat.

The Design space will also be notifying you of the progress of the cut: how many passes to complete your project, and the amount of time remaining to finish your project. This is amazing as it will help you get the progress of your work any time you check on it. That is, in case, you need to carry out other pressing task at hand.

The materials required for this project include Cricut machine (Maker or Expression), 3"X24" Bass wood, rotary blade, painter's tape.

First thing, as usual, is to design your text to be cut on Cricut Design space. There is no room for assumptions here because it will save you time and money too. But if you already know that and you have your design already, it is time to go the task at hand.

1. You have the design in your Cricut design space already, so click Continue.

2. Select the type of material by clicking on Browse All Materials.

3. Type in Bass wood in the materials and choose the type of Bass wood, preferably 1/16 Basswood.

4. Click done. Ensure that you follow the instructions on the cutting window by moving the star wheel (white in color) to the right of the machine. I believe that you still remember why this is important? Then, the materials should be secured to the Strong Grip mat using tape. Of course, the material should not be more 11" wide.

5. Insert the rotary blade to the accessory clamp. By the way, the machine will give a warning if the blade is not inserted.

6. Now, you load the mat into the machine by pressing on the Load/Unload button.

7. The machine will start cutting when you press the flashing Cricut button. It will make an entire pass of the image the machine is going to cut before cutting the full image. Of course, this will take time because of the thickness of the cut. Therefore, you can do other pressing task at hand.

8. Unload the mat by pressing the Load/Unload button which will be blinking when the task is complete.

9. Remove the tape and your material from the mat.

10. Use the weeding tool to remove your design from the whole material gently.

Working on this project would have stirred your creative mind on the many ideas you can accomplish following this approach. Release your creative mind and get working. I am really excited and I hope you are too.

Charming Driftwood Sign

You will need following things

• Wood plank

• Some Paint

• Vinyl

• Piece of rope

Select an appropriate size of wooden piece with some suitable length. As you are using it so it's totally up to you which size you prefer. Draw a shape and image on piece of paper. Place this image on the wooden plank and draw the shape by using paper image as stencil with some prominent marker color. Paint the image or letter with any bright color or with any color of your choice. In final step, add vinyl covering. It is ready to use, now pass some thread, rope or any other hanging material.

Party Decor Medallions

You will need following things

• Records- 45 same size

• Poster board

• Scale

• Scissors

• Adhesive/Glue

• Vintage Milk Caps

• Twine

• Scrapbook

• Scallop Punch

In first step measurements are made and cutting is applied to paper. Fold many papers and cut them in once, paper with measurement of 6,5,4 inches in width for small, medium and large medallions. By holding one end of paper fold it, repeat the folds backward and forth ward. All of the paper strips should be folded in a same way. Now attach all of the strips with the help of glue but in the way they become in the form of seamless strip. Squeeze the strips from the end and pull all of the strips to form it in a shape of a circle. By using glue take the record and attach it from lower portion of paper medallion. Now take 2.5 scallop and fix them with each other. Apply some glue to the center and fix the milk cap and center of the circle. On the back side of center top of medallion attach a twine piece; pass a string in to it, now it is ready for hanging on the wall or in any other place.

Chalkboard Calendar

Required items are

• Wooden board

• Wooden filler

• Scale

- Paints

- Cutter

A large cardboard piece, any used cardboard can be reused. Use some wood filler to fill or fix the holes, if any. Paint the board with any of your favorite or desired colors. By using Silhouette SD cut the chalkboard, and carefully draw some square with exact measurements. Mark the area by using chalk ink markers. Now make some holders by using the Mason jar and pipe clamp. You can assign any sign or add any of tags, and any kind of references to it.

Family Birthday Wooden Board

You will need following things

- Wooden Board

- Chalk Paints

- Paint Brushes

- Finishing Cloths

- Plastic Gloves

- Sandpapers

- Old Rags

• Lettering vinyl

Apply coat of chalk paint to the wooden board, let it dry. Then do another coating of paint for fine look. Give some time like two hours to complete its drying period. Now take some wood finishing cloth. By using old rug wipe all of the extra paint. Then give again some time to get it dry. Designing family members name and counting age numbers style of quoting them is personal choice. Very slightly and carefully use sand paper. Now apply the vinyl, in lettering. Color and design of letter is totally up to you choice.

Vinyl Clock

Needing supplies:

• Vinyl record

• Old Clock machine

• Glue/gum

Vinyl clock project is very interesting. It can be implicated in so much ways. First of all cut the vinyl record in a shape of your choice, square, triangle, flower, circle and in any shape. Set the clock machine in a center of vinyl record. Use glue to fix it right in the center. Vinyl clock is just ready for use. Place it on your desk with by attaching some stand to it or hang it on your wall.

Pallet sign

Amazon now sells pallet wood signs, so no more trying to salvage wood and assemble it just to follow a trend. Pallet wood signs can be purchased in two different sizes by the newest hot Amazon seller called 48×40. The pallet signs come in two different sizes, small and large.

Here is what else you need:

• Scrapbook paper in the colors of your choice

• Mod podge

• Paper trimmer

• Paint brush.

Using your Mod Podge, coat the wood boards and the backside of your triangles. Place the triangles one at a time on the board, coating the top with another thin coat of Mod Podge. Allow your sign to completely dry and then give it a final coat of Mod Podge.

That is it. Last tip, if you are looking for pallet sign ideas, 48×40 has tons of them on the internet.

Ideas For "Etching On Glass And Metal"

Glass Application Projects

Glass application projects are extremely fun and perfect to add some personality to your house and even your car. You will learn to create a variety of projects that you can further customize as you follow the instructions below and have unique designs of your own.

Window Decoration

Materials needed

- "Cricut Maker" or "Cricut Explore"
- Cutting mat

- Orange window cling (non adhesive material that has static cling so it can be easily applied on glass; since it does not have sticky cling like vinyl, make sure you put this on the inner side of the window to protect exposure from external weather).

Step 1

Log into the "Design Space" application and click on the "New Project" button on the top right corner of the screen to view a blank canvas.

Step 2

Click on the "Projects" icon click on the "All Categories" to select "Home Decor" then type in "window" in the search bar.

Step 3

Click on "Customize" to further edit the project to your preference or simply click on the "Make It" button and load the window cling to your "Cricut" machine and follow the instructions on the screen to cut your project and transfer onto the window.

Car Decal

Materials needed

- "Cricut Maker" or "Cricut Explore"
- Cutting mat
- Vinyl
- Transfer tape
- Scrapper

Step 1

Log into the "Design Space" application and click on the "New Project" button on the top right corner of the screen to view a blank canvas.

Step 2

Let's use our own image for this project. Search the web to find the image that you would like and store it on your computer. Now, click on "Upload" icon from the "Designer Panel" on the left of the screen.

Step 3

A screen with "Upload Image" and "Upload Pattern" will be displayed. Click on the "Upload Image" button. Click on "Browse" or simply drag and drop your image on the screen.

Step 4

Your uploaded image will be displayed on the screen and you would be able to select if you would like to upload the image as a simple "single layer" picture or complex "multiple layer" picture. For the decal image below, we will select "simple" and click on "Continue".

Step 5

Save the image as "Print then Cut" image by clicking on the picture on the left then clicking "Save" at the bottom right of the screen.

Step 6

Select the uploaded image and click on "Insert Images" then edit as needed.

Step 7

Click on "Customize" to further edit the project to your preference or simply click on the "Make It" button and load the window cling to your "Cricut" machine and follow the instructions on the screen to cut the design.

Step 8

Carefully remove the excess material from the sheet. To easily paste your decal on the car window without stretching the pieces, put the transfer tape on top of the cut design. After you have cleaned the car window, slowly peel the paper backing on the vinyl from one end to the other in a rolling motion to ensure even placement. Now, use the scraper tool on top of the transfer tape to remove any bubbles and then just peel off the transfer tape. And you are all set!

Holiday Mirror Decoration

Materials needed

- "Cricut Maker" or "Cricut Explore"
- Cutting mat
- Vinyl
- Transfer tape
- Scrapper

Step 1

Log into the "Design Space" application and click on the "New Project" button on the top right corner of the screen to view a blank canvas.

Step 2

Click on the "Images" icon and type in "reindeer" in the search bar. Select a picture that you like and click on "Insert Image".

Step 3

Now type in "wreath" in the search bar and scroll down to find the image used in this project. Click on it and a small icon will be added to the "Insert Image" bar at the bottom of the screen. Click on "Insert Images" at the bottom of the screen.

Step 4

Edit the design and click on the "Fill" icon from the "Edit Bar" at the top of the screen to select "Print" and then change the color of the deer to red. Click on the lock icon at the bottom left of the deer image to adjust the image inside the wreath.

Step 5

Select the entire design and click on "Group" icon under the "Layers panel". Then click on "Save" to save the project.

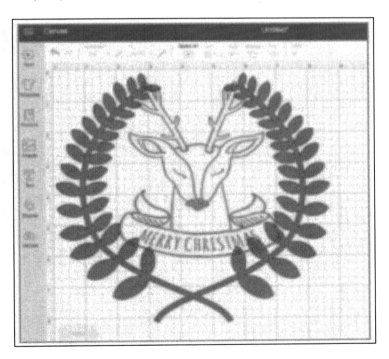

Step 6

The design is ready to be cut. Simply click on the "Make It" button and load the vinyl sheet to your "Cricut" machine and follow the instructions on the screen to cut the design.

Step 7

Carefully remove the excess vinyl from the sheet and put the transfer tape on top of the cut design. After you have cleaned the mirror, slowly peel the paper backing on the vinyl from one end to the other in a rolling motion to ensure even placement. Now, use the scraper tool on top of the transfer tape to remove any bubbles and then just peel off the transfer tape.

Wine Glass Decoration

Materials needed

- "Cricut Maker" or "Cricut Explore"
- Cutting mat
- Vinyl (gold)
- Transfer tape
- Scrapper
- Wine glasses

Step 1

Log into the "Design Space" application and click on the "New Project" button on the top right corner of the screen to view a blank canvas.

Step 2

Let's use text for this project. Click on "Text" from the "Designs Panel" on the left of the screen and type in "WINE O'clock" or any other phrase you may like.

Step 3

For the image below, the font "Anna's Fancy Lettering – Hannah" in purple as shown in the picture below was selected. But you can let your creativity take over this step and choose any color or font that you like. Select and copy-paste your image for the number of times you want to print your design.

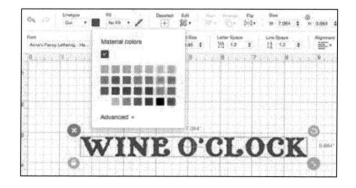

Step 4

Click on "Save" to save the project then click on the "Make It" button and load the vinyl sheet to your "Cricut" machine and follow the instructions on the screen to cut the design.

Step 5

Carefully remove the excess vinyl from the sheet. To easily paste your design on the wine glass without stretching the pieces, put the transfer tape on top of the cut design. After you have cleaned the surface, slowly peel the paper backing on the vinyl from one end to the other in a rolling motion to ensure even placement. Now, use the scraper tool on top of the transfer tape to remove any bubbles and then just peel off the transfer tape.

Ideas For " Various And Other Projects"

Now that you have learnt how to set up and use your Cricut machine, it is time to actually use it to bring those fantastic projects you have always dreamed about to life. We have tried to include projects diverse enough to provide an exhaustive view of the capabilities of your Cricut machine and to give you a good idea of what possibilities exist in expressing your yet untapped creativity and undiscovered potential.

Felt Roses

Materials needed:

- SVG files with 3D flower design
- Felt Sheets
- Fabric Grip Mat

- Glue Gun

STEPS:

- First of all, upload your Flower SVG Graphics into the Cricut design space as explained in the "Tips" section. ("How to import images into Cricut Design Space)

- Having placed the image in the project, select it, right-click and click "Ungroup". This allows you to resize each flower independent of the others. Since you are using felt, it is recommended that each of the flowers are at least 6 inches in size.

- Create several copies of the flowers, as many as you wish, selecting the colors you want in the Color Sync Panel (by dragging and dropping the images on to the color you would want them to be cut on). Immediately you're through with that, click on "Make it" on the Cricut design space.

- Click on "Continue". After your Cricut Maker is connected and registered, under the "materials" options, select "Felt".

- If your rotary blade is not in the machine, insert it. Next, on the Fabric Grip Mat, place the first felt sheet (in order of color), then, load them into your Cricut Maker. Press the "cut" button when this is done.

- After they are cut, begin to roll the cut flowers one by one. Do this from the outside in. Make sure that you do not roll them too tight. Use the picture as a guide.

- Apply Hot Glue on the circle right in the middle and press the felt flowers that you rolled up on the glue. Hold this in place and do not let it go until the glue binds it.

- Wait for the glue to dry, and your roses are ready for use.

Custom Coasters

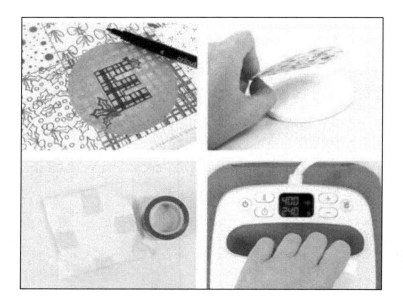

Materials needed:

- Free Pattern Templates
- Monogram Design (in Design Space)
- Cardstock or Printing Paper
- Butcher Paper
- Lint-free towel
- Round Coaster Blanks
- LightGrip Mat
- EasyPress 2 (6" x 7" recommended)

- EasyPress Mat
- Infusible Ink Pens
- Heat Resistant Tape
- Cricut BrightPad (optional) for easier tracing

STEPS:

- In Cricut Design Space, open the monogram design. You can click "Customize" and choose the designs that you want to cut out or just go ahead and cut out all the letters.

- Click on "Make It".

- On the page displayed, click on "Mirror Image" to make the image mirrored. This must be done whenever you are using infusible ink. For your material, choose "Cardstock". Then, place your cardstock on the mat and load it into the machine; then press the "Cut" button on the Cricut machine.

- After the Cricut machine is done cutting, unload it and remove the done monograms from the mat.

- Trace the designs onto the cut-out. If you have a Cricut BrightPad, you can use it to carry out this step much more easily, as it will make the trace lines easier to identify. Tracing should be done using Cricut Infusible Ink Pens.

- Use the lint-free towel to wipe the coaster. Ensure that no residue is left behind to prevent any marks being left on the blank.

- Make the design centered on the face down coaster.

- Get a piece of butcher paper which is about an inch larger on each side of the coaster and place on top of the design.

- Tape this butcher paper onto the coaster using heat resistant tape, to hold the design fast.

- Set the temperature of your EasyPress to 400 degrees and set the timer to 240 seconds.

- Place another butcher paper piece on your EasyPress mat, set the coaster on top of it, face up.

- Place another piece of butcher paper on top of these. Place the already preheated EasyPress on top of the coaster and start the timer.

- Lightly hold the EasyPress in place (without moving) or leave it in place right on the coaster – if on a perfectly flat surface – till the timer goes off.

- After this is done, gently remove the EasyPress 2 then turn it off.

- The coaster will be very hot, so you should leave it to get cool before you touch it. When it is cool, you can peel the design off of it.

Customized Doormat

Materials needed:

- Cricut Machine
- Scrap cardstock (The color does not matter)

- Coir mat (18" x 30")
- Outdoor acrylic paint
- Vinyl stencil
- Transfer tape
- Flat round paintbrush
- Cutting mat (12" x 24")

STEPS:

- Create your design in Cricut Design Space. You can also download an SVG design of your choice and import into Cricut Design Space. Make sure that your design is the right size; resize it to ensure that this is so.

- Next, you are to cut the stencil. You do this by clicking "Make it" in Cricut Design Space when you are done with the design. After this, you select "Cardstock" as the material. Then, you press the "Cut" button on the Cricut machine.

- When this is done, remove the stencil from the machine and weed.

- Next, on the reverse side of the stencil, apply spray glue. After this, attach the stencil to the doormat, exactly where you want your design to be; then, pick up the letter bits left on the cutting mat and glue them to their places in the stencil on the doormat.

- The next step is to mask the parts of the doormat which you do not want to paint on. You can do this using painters' plastic.

- Now, it's time to spray-paint your stencil on the doormat. Keeping the paint can about 5 inches away from the doormat, spray up and down, keeping the can pointed straight through the stencil. If it is at an angle, the paint will get under the stencil and ruin your design. Spray the entire stencil 2-3 times to make sure that you do not miss any part and that the paint is even.

- You're just about done! Now, remove the masking plastic and the stencil and leave the doormat for about one hour to get dry.

T-Shirts (Vinyl, Iron On)

To make custom t-shirts using your Cricut machine, you will need to use iron-on or heat transfer vinyl. Ensure that you choose a color that contrasts and matches well with your t-shirt.

Materials needed:

- Cricut Machine
- T-shirt
- Iron on or heat transfer vinyl

- Fine point blade and light grip mat
- Weeding tools
- EasyPress (regular household iron works fine too, with a little extra work)
- Small towel and Parchment paper

STEPS:

- In preparing for this project, Cricut recommends that you prewash the cloth without using any fabric softener before applying the iron-on or heat transfer vinyl on it. Ensure that your T-shirt is dry and ready before you proceed.

- On Cricut Design Space, create your design or import your SVG as described in the section on importing images.

- If you are using an SVG file, select it and click on "Insert Images". When you do this, the image will appear in the Design Space canvas area.

- Then, you need to resize the image to fit the T-shirt. To do this, select all the elements, then set the height and width in the edit panel area, or simply drag the handle on the lower right corner of the selection.

- After this is done, select all the layers and click "Attach" at the bottom of the "Layers" panel, so that the machine cuts everything just as it is displayed on the canvas area.

- You can preview your design using Design Space's templates. You access this by clicking the icon called "templates" on the left panel of Design Space's canvas. There, you can choose what surface on which to visualize your design. Choose the color of your vinyl and of the T-shirt so you can see how it will look once completed.

- Once you are satisfied with the appearance of your design, click "Make It". If you have not connected your machine, you will be prompted to do so.

- When the "Prepare" page shows, there is a "Mirror" option on the left panel. Ensure that you turn this on. This will make the machine cut it in reverse, as the top is the part that goes on to the T-shirt. Click "Continue".

- Next, you are to select the material. When using the Cricut Maker, you will do this in Cricut Design Space. Choose "Everyday Iron-On". On Cricut Explore Air, you select the material using the smart set dial on the machine. Set this dial to "Iron-On".

- Now, it's time to cut. To cut vinyl (and other such light materials), you should use the light-grip blue mat. Place the iron-on vinyl on the mat with the dull side facing up. Ensure that there are no bubbles on the vinyl; you can do this using the scraper.

- Install the fine point blade in the Cricut machine, then load the mat with the vinyl on it by tapping the small arrow on the machine. Then, press the "make it" button. When the machine is done cutting the vinyl, Cricut Design Space will notify you. When this happens, unload the mat.

- With the cutting done, it is time to weed. This must be done patiently, so that you do not cut out the wrong parts. Therefore, you should have the design open as a guide.

- After weeding, it is finally time to transfer the vinyl to the T-shirt. Before this, ensure that you have prewashed the T-shirt without fabric softener, as mentioned at the beginning of this project.

- To transfer the design, you can use the EasyPress or a regular pressing iron. Using a pressing iron may be a little more difficult, but it is certainly doable. Before you transfer, ensure that you have the EasyPress mat or a towel behind the material on to which you want to transfer the design so as to allow the material to be pressed harder against the heat.

- Set the EasyPress to the temperature recommended on the Cricut heat guide for your chosen heat-transfer material and base material. For a combination of iron-on vinyl and cotton, the temperature should be set to 330°F. After preheating the EasyPress, get rid of wrinkles on the T-shirt and press the EasyPress on it for about 5 seconds. Then, place the design on the T-shirt and apply pressure for 30 seconds. After this, apply the EasyPress on the back of the T-shirt for about 15 seconds.

- If you're using a pressing iron, the process is similar; only that you need to preheat the iron to max heat and place a thin cloth on the design, such that the iron does not have direct contact with the design or the T-shirt. This will prevent you from burning the T-shirt.

- Wait for the design to cool off a bit, then peel it off while it is still a little warm.

- Ensure that you wait for at least 24 hours after this before washing the T-shirt. When you do wash it, be sure to dry it inside out. Also, do not bleach the T-shirt.

3d Paper Flowers (Paper)

Materials needed:

- Cricut Machine
- Cricut mat
- Colored scrapbook paper
- Hot glue gun and glue sticks

STEPS:

- To make flowers, you need an appropriate shape for the petals. To make such a shape, you can combine three ovals of equal size. To create an oval, select the circle tool, then create a circle. Then click the unlock button at the bottom of the shape. Once this is done, you can reshape the circle to form an oval.

- Duplicate this oval twice and rotate each duplicate a little, keeping the bottom at the same point, as shown in the picture.

- Select all three ovals and weld them together to get your custom petal shape. For each large flower, you need 12 petals – each one about 3 inches long, while for each small flower, you need 8 petals – each one about 2 inches long. For each flower, you

452

also need a circle shape for the base of about the same width as each petal. Arrange the petals and base circle shape in Cricut Design Studio.

- Set your material to cardstock on Design Space or on the machine, depending on your machine, then cut the petals out.

- After you cut out the petals, remove them and cut a slit about half an inch long in the bottom of each one. Place a bit of glue on the left side and glue the right side over the glue for each petal.

- The next thing to do is to place the petals on the circle base. For large flowers, you need three circles of four petals each. For small flowers, you need five circles on the outside and three on the inside. Put a bit of hot glue on the petal and add to the circle as described above.

- For the center of the flowers, search Cricut Access for "flower" and chose shapes with several small petals. Cut these out using a different color of cardstock and glue to the center of the flowers.

Luminaries

Materials needed:

- Luminary Graphic (From a Cricut Project)
- Sugar Skull (SVG File)
- Cricut Explore Air or Cricut Maker
- Cardstock Sampler
- Scoring Stylus
- Glue Stick
- Battery-Operated Tea Light

STEPS:

- The first step is to open your Luminary graphic on the Design Space.

- Then go ahead to upload the SVG file of your Sugar Skull and adjust its size to around 3.25" high. After doing that, move the Sugar Skull to the bigger part of the Luminary graphic (in the middle of the two score lines) and center-align it.

- Select the Sugar Skull and the Luminary Graphic and then go ahead and click on "Weld".

- Try selecting every graphic on the design space and click on "Attach." Then copy and paste the selected graphics on the same page (duplication).

- Select "Make It" at the topmost right-hand corner, and then ensure everything is positioned correctly. Click on

- "Continue." If you notice the files being cut on two different mats, just move them back together on one single mat by simply clicking on these three dots located at the graphic corner.

- Select "Light Cardstock" under the "Materials" menu, and then start loading the Mat and Cut. Also ensure that your Scoring Stylus is in Clamp A. This will automatically change your machine settings from scoring to cutting.

- When the cut-out is done, fold it along the Score lines. Then start gluing the small Flap to the interior part of the lantern's back.

- Switch on the Battery-Operated Tea Light, and then place your lantern on top of it.

Shamrock Earrings

Materials needed:

- Cricut Maker
- Earring (from a Cricut Project)
- Rotary Wheel
- Knife Blade
- FabricGrip Mat
- StrongGrip Mat
- Weeder Tool
- Cricut Leather
- Scraper Tool
- Adhesive
- Pebbled-Faux Leather
- Earring Hooks

STEPS:

- First, open the Cricut Project (Earring). You can now either click on "Make It" or "Customize" to edit it.

- Once you've selected one, click on "Continue."

- Immediately the Cut page pops up, select your material and wait for the "Load" tools and Mat to appear.

- Make your Knife blade your cutting tool in clamp B. This will be used on the Leather.

- On the StrongGrip Mat, place the Leather and make sure it's facing down. Then load the Mat into the machine and tap the "Cut" flashing button.

- When the scoring has been done, go back to the cutting tool and change it to Rotary Wheel so that you can use it on the Faux Leather.

- Similarly, place your Faux leather on your FabricGrip Mat, facing down. Then load the Mat into the machine and tap the "Cut" flashing button.

- Take away all the items on the Mat with your Scraper tool. Be careful with the small fringes though.

- Make a hole on the top circle by making use of the Weeder tool. Make sure the hole is large enough to make the Earring hooks fit in.

- If necessary, you may have to twist the hook's end with the pliers to fit them in.

- Close them up after you have looped it inside the hole that was made inside the Earring.

458

- Finally, you should glue the Shamrock to the surface of the Earring with adhesive. Wait for it to dry before using.

Valentine's Day Classroom Cards

Materials needed:

- Cricut Maker
- Card Designs (Write Stuff Coloring)
- Cricut Design Space
- Dual Scoring Wheel
- Pens
- Cardstock

- Crayons
- Shimmer Paper

STEPS:

- Open the Card Designs (Write Stuff Coloring) on the Design Space, and then click on "Make it" or "Customize" to make edits.

- When all the changes have been done, Cricut will request you to select a material. Select Cardstock for the Cards and Shimmer Paper for the Envelopes.

- Cricut will send you a notification when you need to change the pen colors while creating the Card, and then it will start carving the Card out automatically.

- You will be prompted later on to change the blade because of the Double Scoring Wheel. It is advisable to use the Double Scoring Wheel with Shimmer Paper; they both work best together.

- When the scoring has been finished, replace the Scoring Wheel with the prior blade.

- After that, fold the flaps at the Score lines in the direction of the paper's white side, and then attach the Side Tabs to the exterior of the Bottom Tab by gluing them together.

- You may now write "From:" and "To:" before placing the Crayons into the Slots.

- Place the Cards inside the Envelopes and tag it with a sharp object.

Conclusion

Expressions and artworks have made some amazing progress in the past decade, and couple of things demonstrate this reality more than the Cricut machine. As you have seen, this machine is all that you have to turn any bit of paper, any take home gift, or any placemat into the craft you had always wanted.

Regardless of whether you are arranging a gathering, a supper, or any kind of occasion get together, you know you need the solicitations and the cute gifts to be great. You know you long for your visitors strolling into the room and seeing something that blows their mind.

You need to have customized, visitor prepared cards sitting out and around your table, and you need to welcome your visitors into your home with just the best sitting out and sitting tight for them. What's more, you know you can achieve the majority of this with the Cricut Printer... you simply need to figure out how.

Everything necessary is a couple of provisions and some simple guidelines, and you can influence everything without exception you to can envision. You don't need to be a specialist, and you don't need to be great at makes. Give the Cricut a chance to do the diligent work for you, and love the outcomes!

Manufactured by Amazon.ca
Bolton, ON

15296069R00254